Walter Gregory in Barcelona, August 1937.
This photo was taken after the Battle of Brunete and
before the first Aragon offensive.

THE SHALLOW GRAVE
A Memoir of the Spanish Civil War

WALTER GREGORY

Foreword by Jack Jones CH

Edited by
David Morris and Anthony Peters

LONDON
VICTOR GOLLANCZ LTD
1986

First published in Great Britain 1986
by Victor Gollancz Ltd,
14 Henrietta Street, London WC2E 8QJ

© Walter Gregory, David Morris and Anthony Peters 1986

Maps drawn by Don Sargeant

British Library Cataloguing in Publication Data
Gregory, Walter
   The shallow grave: a memoir of the Spanish Civil War.
   1. Spain—History—Civil War, 1936-1939—
Personal narratives
   I. Title   II. Morris, David   III. Peters, Anthony
   946.081'092'4   DP269.9

   ISBN 0-575-03790-3

Typeset at The Spartan Press Limited, Lymington, Hants.
and printed in Great Britain by
St Edmundsbury Press, Bury St Edmunds, Suffolk
Illustrations originated and printed by Thomas Campone, Southampton

This book is dedicated to the memory

of

BERNARD GEORGE WINFIELD

of

Nottingham

A true friend and loyal comrade who
gave his life in the fight for democracy
at Teruel on 20 January 1938

Voluntario de la Libertad

A brave soldier in the ranks of
XVth International Brigade

There's a valley in Spain called Jarama,
That's a place that we all know so well,
For 'tis here that we wasted our manhood,
And most of our old age as well.

From this valley they tell us we're leaving,
But don't hasten to bid us adieu,
For e'en though we make our departure,
We'll be back in an hour or two.

Oh we're proud of our British Battalion,
And the marathon record it's made,
Please do us this little favour,
And take this last word to Brigade.

You'll never be happy with strangers,
They would not understand you as we,
So remember the Jarama Valley
And the old men who wait patiently.

ALEC McDADE

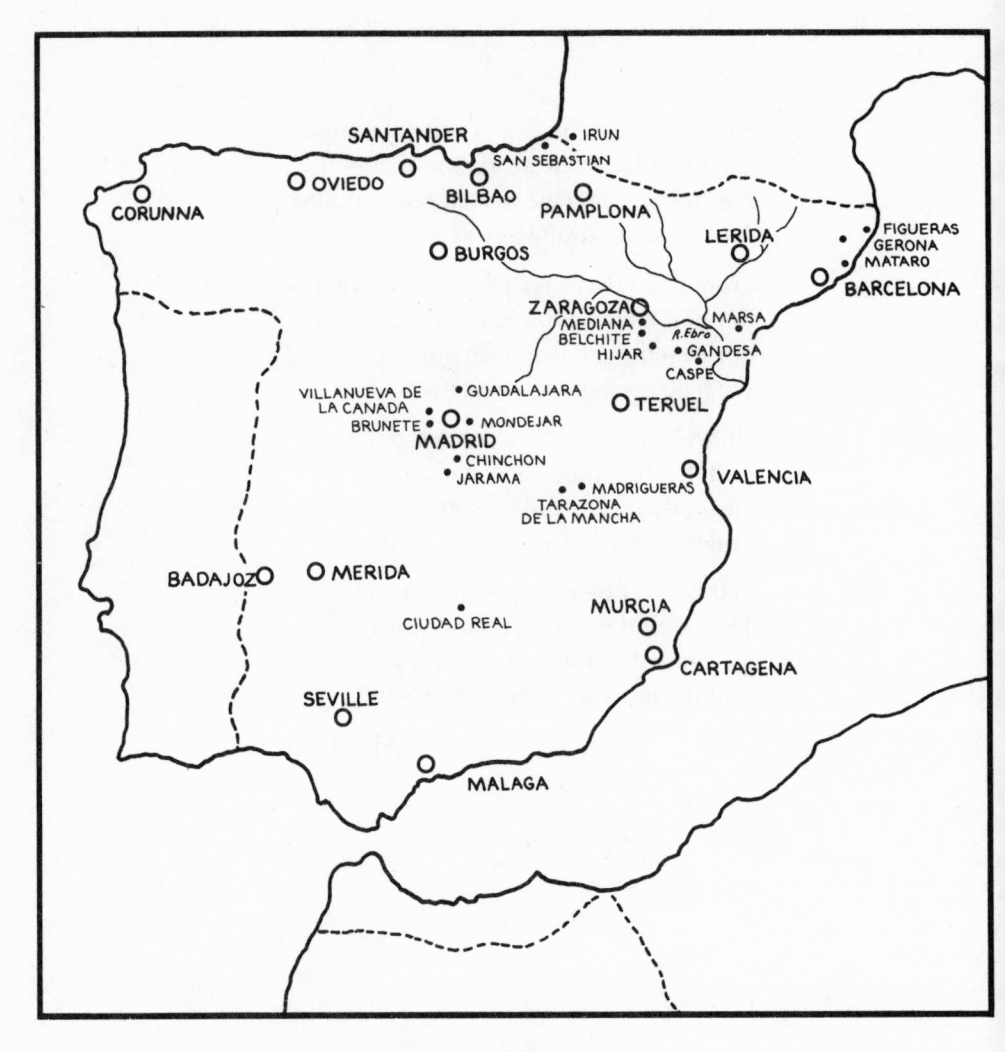

Places mentioned in the text
(Rivers other than the Ebro are not shown)

Contents

Illustrations

9

ILLUSTRATIONS

facing page 155

The Foreign Office's request for reimbursement for Walter's repatriation
from Franco's prison

MAPS

Foreword

Here is a dramatic and human story of a brave man: a vivid account of the life of a lad from Lincoln who played a noble part in the civil war in Spain. From a background of drab streets and a weary search for work in the 1920s and 30s, lightened somewhat by his deep political convictions, participation in the 1934 Hunger March and clashes with the blackshirts, Walter Gregory went on to serve in the International Brigade. The book is one which should command the attention of students of history, for those who so often ask the question, 'What motivated the international volunteers in Spain?' will find some part of the answer here.

A saga of movement and action, of self-sacrifice and bitter struggle, it is recounted with modesty and a degree of humour. In a sense it is a page torn from history, a valuable page, portraying the real life and spirit of one man who left home and loved ones to serve democracy and freedom in a foreign land. The events recorded took place within a period when the harsh forces of Fascism were advancing throughout Europe. The British Government, which might have been expected to lend a hand to another democratic government, dithered and procrastinated, and by its policy of 'non-intervention' encouraged Fascist aggression.

The call to build the International Brigades was made in response to the desperate circumstances facing the elected Government of the Spanish Republic and its people. There was urgent need for courageous and determined men to give strength and succour to the forces of the Republic. From all parts of the world ordinary folk responded, seeing it as a matter of honour to defend democracy. It is surely right to record as much as possible of the human endeavour involved, and it is especially from that point of view that I warmly welcome this publication.

Despite many setbacks, suffering, and the death of comrades, Walter Gregory never lost his commitment. There are no complaints of privation in this story, yet he experienced it in full measure. Wounded many times and, in the end, taken prisoner, he typifies all that was best in the epic story

of the International Brigades. From a personal point of view I feel proud and privileged to have served with such men. The conditions under which the volunteers toiled and fought were intensely difficult and harsh, but courage, loyalty and decency were manifest. The volunteers battled for a noble purpose, subsequently vindicated by the rebirth of democracy in Spain. The proud and gallant story of the International Brigades, in consequence, must surely occupy an honourable place in the archives of world progress.

The skilled assistance of David Morris and Anthony Peters has made this book possible and I am grateful to them. It is splendid reading and I am very glad that it has been written. I compliment Walter Gregory and his two colleagues for making available such a stirring and interesting account.

JACK JONES
1985

Preface

It has taken me the best part of half a century to get round to recording my experiences in the Spanish Civil War, for no sooner had it ended than we were once again plunged into further preparations for war. But no other issue in my lifetime was to make such an impact upon public sympathies in Britain as did the Spanish Civil War. Very many people from all walks of life were involved in the campaign to support the Republican Government: trade unionists, political party members, the co-operative guilds, trade and labour associations, chapels and churches. All of these set aside their differences and united not only to collect food parcels to be sent to supporters of the Republic but also to raise funds to provide ambulances complete with staff and equipment. Thousands showed their support for the defenders of Spanish democracy in its fight against Fascism without waiting for nationally organized campaigns to appear. The numbers prepared to go out to Spain as doctors, nurses and soldiers were limited by the funds available to pay their expenses and to make some small provision to support the families they left behind. The British people provided over two and a half thousand *voluntarios de la libertad* but these could easily have been far more, had money been available. At home campaigns supporting the struggle entered into by the elected government of Spain drew forth volunteers and the volunteers in Spain encouraged the people back home to be part of that struggle.

W. G.

Acknowledgements

I have a great many people to thank and without whose advice and assistance this book could never have appeared. I have to thank my old comrade of the Spanish battlefields, Bert Hartwell, and his wife, Eve, whose insistence that I should return to Spain in 1981, in a party organized by Bill Alexander, provided the motivation I needed to commit my recollections to paper. I also have to thank Bill for introducing me to Christopher Cook, the producer of a BBC television documentary made in Spain when we revisited the former army bases and battlefields at Jarama, Brunete, Aragon, Teruel and Gandesa. Without the kindness and inexhaustible patience shown towards me by Chris during extensive filming and, but for the screening of that programme, 'A Return to the Battlefields', on BBC2 in February 1982, I would never have been dragged out of obscurity. I must also express my sincere thanks to another old comrade who saw service with the International Brigade and was wounded in the Ebro Battle, August 1938, who later became General Secretary of the Transport and General Workers Union – Jack Jones, for so readily and generously agreeing to write the Foreword.

My thanks also go to my son, David, who kindly read every page of the manuscript as it passed through its many formative stages with the instruction to comment as though he was marking his school papers. This he did, and his suggestions have been of enormous help to me.

Most of all I shall always be indebted to Dave Morris and Tony Peters of the Department of Public Sector Administration, Sheffield City Polytechnic, who literally burst into my quiet retirement and committed me to this literary effort before I had time to say 'No' or to hide behind a plea of old age and failing memory. Without their enormous efforts and diligence this book would never have been completed.

Finally, I am indebted to the Spanish people I met both during the Civil War and later. Their courage and loyalty under atrocious conditions were quite incredible. They made an impression on me that has lasted all my

life. I was privileged to have been associated with them during their trials and I am prouder of my battle scars than I could ever be of a chestful of medals.

W.G.
Nottingham 1985

We owe our thanks and appreciation to many people who have made our task both more pleasurable and less arduous than it would have been without their help and encouragement. Our first and greatest debt is to Walter Gregory without whose patience, enthusiasm and skill as a raconteur this book could never have been written. To Walter's wife, Gladys, we extend our sincere thanks for letting us 'borrow' her husband on numerous occasions and for uncomplainingly allowing us to disrupt her life by the many demands we made upon Walter. Chris Cook facilitated our initial contact with Walter and by so doing created the foundation for the book. Jeanette Davis, Ann Rees and Jean Smith performed the difficult and tedious task of transcribing our taped conversations and Audrey Roberts and Gwen Escott typed the manuscript. Margot Madin and Laura Tolley of the Eric Mensforth Library, Sheffield City Polytechnic, gave invaluable help in tracing the many important sources of secondary material that we needed. Our Head of Department, Bob Haigh, never failed to give us constant encouragement and his oft repeated question, 'Isn't that thing written yet?', which was invariably accompanied by the comment, 'It's taking longer to write than *War and Peace*', served to spur us on to greater efforts.

Special thanks are due to Jack Jones, for not only taking time out from a busy schedule to read the manuscript but also for writing so pertinent a foreword.

Elfreda Powell of Victor Gollancz provided us with cheerful encouragement at every stage as the mauscript was transformed into a book, and our acknowledgements would be incomplete were we not to record our appreciation of her efforts.

Finally, we must record our deepest appreciation to our wives, Sheila and Alison, and to our children, Richard and Sarah, for so readily tolerating the many occasions on which we 'deserted' them so that we could complete this book.

D.S.M.
A.R.P.
Sheffield 1985

THE SHALLOW GRAVE

I

Journey to the Front Line

Setting off for Spain on Monday 22nd December 1936, I was like a holidaymaker going abroad for the first time. Never before had I travelled further from Nottingham than London, for such holidays as I had enjoyed as a youngster had always been spent with grandparents in Newark or Peterborough, and here I was going to Spain to fight the Fascists.

It had been the fifth month of the war when I was approached by Clarence Mason, the paid Communist Party organizer for the Nottingham area, to ask if I would like to be a volunteer for the International Brigades. Not that volunteers were hard to come by, but the Party had placed restrictions on eligibility. Volunteers had to be twenty-one or over – as the death in action of a minor might have provided a ready means for the capitalist press to criticize Party activities – and unmarried – as there was little likelihood of a widow receiving any form of financial support from the Spanish government were her husband to be killed. Disability pensions were also thought to be unlikely to be forthcoming. So volunteers were sought who had few dependants as financial aid for them would have to come from the proceeds of relief work, and the amounts likely to be distributed would not be more than a few shillings a week. Clarence approached me because I was single, both of my sisters were in regular employment, and my mother was receiving a widow's pension.

Hardly had Clarence finished asking me if I would be prepared to go to Spain than I was saying, 'Yes. I'll go. When do I set off? How do I get there?' I was wild with excitement, I was going to Spain, I was going to fight for democracy, I was going to fight against Fascism. Here was somebody really asking *me* to do something important. Not just asking me to canvass for somebody else to be elected to Parliament or to a local council, but actually asking *me* to go and fight against a Fascist dictatorship! I was over the moon, I thought it was absolutely marvellous.

Looking back now to the summer of 1936, it is astonishing how little I knew of Spain. I did not appreciate its form of government at all and was

content simply to label it as 'democratic'. I had no inkling of the corruption which characterized the governments of the Second Republic and no real knowledge of the parliamentary parties and extra-parliamentary groups which were engaged in the struggle for power. The actual causes of the outbreak of the Civil War were barely obvious to me except in terms of the broadest generality: 'The Fascists are trying to kill a democracy.' In my ignorance I was probably typical of the average British working-class man and yet, despite the widespread lack of knowledge of Spain, I cannot recall any other international or domestic political issue having such an explosive impact upon the British working-class as that produced by the Spanish Civil War. Nor can I explain why this was so. Not Manchuria, not Abyssinia, not the great oppressive strides being taken by Fascism in Europe, nor the miseries of the depression at home came anywhere near to rivalling Spain as a focus for working-class attention and indignation.

Within days of the Civil War starting in Spain, the British Communist Party had doubled and trebled its efforts to establish a United Front Against Fascism or, as our European comrades termed it, a Popular Front. Nobody in the Communist Party saw the Spanish Civil War as just another civil war, Spain was different, Spain was about opposing the growth and spread of Fascism by armed force, of meeting Fascist aggression with aggression and of ensuring the safety of democracy in the face of the Fascist challenge. In Britain, the Communist Party's efforts fell on barren ground as far as the two major political parties were concerned. The Conservatives could hardly have been expected to offer resistance to the right-wing Nationalist insurrection against a left-of-centre government in Spain, but the Labour Party proved to be a major disappointment. Perhaps the Labour Party was still smarting from the ineffectual way it had responded to the domestic situation since the General Strike, but more probably a significant number of Labour politicians felt that their party had nothing to gain and much to lose by associating itself with the appeal of the numerically small Communist Party which was viewed with suspicion, if not open hostility, by most people in Britain. Likewise, the distrust of the Communist Party by the trade union movement seemed sufficient to ensure that the Party's call for a United Front received but a cursory examination before being rejected.

The Comintern, however, lost no time in taking the decision to organize international brigades to go to the support of the Republican forces in Spain: a decision seen by the British Communist Party as a rallying-point for the entire British and European working-class. But the

British Communist Party's parlous finances and organization meant that many British subjects were fighting with the Republican forces in Spain several months before volunteers selected by the Party had made their way across the Pyrénées. Already the first person from Nottingham had made his own way out to Spain to join the Republican forces: Jim Feeney was a long-standing and very active member of the Labour Party and first saw action with that small group of British volunteers fighting on the Córdoba Front.

I am now ashamed to admit that the exhilaration I felt at being asked to volunteer swept from my mind all thoughts of my responsibilities to my widowed mother. Never for one moment did I stop to wonder how she would manage when I threw up my job at the brewery and went to Spain. I did not consider how she would make ends meet with the few shillings a week which she would receive from the relief fund to supplement her pension, nor did I stop to think of what would become of her should I be in Spain for any length of time, or what would happen to her were I to be killed or disabled. All such thoughts, to my shame, never entered my head. I thought of nothing but getting to Spain. (As things later turned out mother received about ten shillings a week from the relief fund throughout my time in Spain, but I was never able to supplement this token amount from my army pay, as I was not allowed to send money home, nor did the Spanish government make any arrangements to 'dock' my pay so that a part of it could be forwarded directly to her.)

But breaking the news of my departure to my mother had been difficult. She was astounded at what she considered to be my stupidity in going to fight in another nation's war. Still being able to recall vividly the horrors of the First World War she assumed that the war in Spain would simply be a repeat of its slaughter, but, having struggled unsuccessfully against my political involvement for so long, she came to accept the inevitability of my going surprisingly quickly. My younger sister, Kathleen, however, was even more anxious for my safety than my mother. Kathleen had been reading newspaper accounts of the savagery current in both the Nationalist and Republican controlled areas of Spain in the wake of the insurrection, and had no doubts as to the brutal nature of the fighting in which I would be involved. But like my mother, she realized my determination to go.

Having broken the news to my family my next task had been to obtain a passport, but the deposit required by the Foreign Office was far more than I could pay. However, Clarence Mason assured me that he would make arrangements to get me safely to Spain without the need for any documentation.

So, three days before Christmas, I arrived at the Midland Station in Nottingham, bursting with excitement, and joined the other passengers waiting on the platform, among them my local member of parliament, Arthur Hayday. We knew one another quite well and I stood near him hoping that he might glance up from his morning newspaper. What did he read that day which so captured his attention? No doubt he read that the rebel generals in Spain had successfully broadened their front by the capture of Boadilla to the west of Madrid, that the Republican militias had failed to dislodge the Fascist insurgents from University City and that in one well-timed thrust Moorish units of Franco's army had penetrated to the Plaza de España deep in the heart of the capital. What did Arthur make of the view that Madrid was likely to fall over the Christmastide? I was never to know for when the train pulled into the station Arthur made his way straight to the nearest first-class coach and I travelled south alone, musing upon the incongruity of a parliamentary representative of the Labour Party making use of first-class facilities. So when I had placed my small suitcase on the luggage rack above my head and settled myself in a window-seat on the train I was in a light-hearted mood.

When Clarence had handed me my railway ticket to London he had given me further instructions. On arrival I was to make my way to King Street, at the back of Covent Garden market, where the Communist Party headquarters were, and to introduce myself to Johnny Campbell, a veteran party worker with a formidable reputation. By midday, along with five other men of roughly my own age or perhaps a shade older, I was being interviewed by Johnny. One of the group could speak some French so he was put in charge of us for the next stage of our journey. We were told to spend the afternoon sightseeing (but separately), and report to Victoria Station later in the evening when we would be given the rail and boat tickets to get us to Paris, and a small amount of French francs for food and drink.

When we gathered at Victoria Station it was explained to us that, ostensibly, we were off on a day trip to Dunkirk, for which no passport was necessary. We were told to remain together at all times on the journey to Paris but to try to create the impression that we were not closely associated and had simply struck up an acquaintance during our travels; this so that we would not attract the attention of the police who, because of the non-interventionist policies of the British and French governments, were keeping a sharp watch for groups of young men making their way south. We caught the midnight boat from Dover. The crossing was rough and we had to grab what sleep we could on the wooden benches of the boat. Early

in the morning we arrived at Dunkirk, tired and tense, and from there we caught the train to Arras. At Arras we changed trains, and at Amiens changed trains again, and finally, in the early afternoon, we pulled into the Gare du Nord in Paris. From there we had to make our separate ways to the Bureau des Syndicats which was the assembly-point for volunteers from all over Europe. I decided to take a taxi, as my total lack of French would probably have meant that I would have been wandering around Paris until long after the conflict in Spain had ended! Without my having to say a word, the taxi-driver sped me to my destination; I must have looked like so many others who had made the same journey before me.

The Bureau des Syndicats looked no different from any other office except that it was a scene of feverish activity and a babble of different languages. I cannot now recall any particular individual in the Paris office, although I have been told that its activities were under the direction of a Yugoslav comrade who later became famous under the name of Tito. In the existing chaos I found someone who spoke English and who gave me a railway ticket to Perpignan, instructed me to go immediately to the Gare d'Austerlitz and take the evening train to Marseilles, where I had to change trains again. Once more I was asked to be discreet in my contacts with fellow volunteers. Again, I used a taxi to take me through the gathering gloom of a late winter afternoon, thus eating still further into the small supply of francs with which I had been provided at King Street.

The journey from Paris to Marseilles was one which I should not care to repeat. The train was bursting at the seams with people returning home for Christmas or taking a holiday. My compartment was crowded with troops going on leave and it was impossible for me to squeeze comfortably into the small remaining space, so I spent the greater part of the journey standing in the corridor with my small suitcase between my feet and being buffeted about as people moved up and down the train as it travelled southward through the night. I was left to reflect that I had missed the opportunity to see the sights of Paris. Paris to me was two railway stations and two rapid taxi journeys which had left me unaware of its splendours.

The train from Marseilles to Perpignan, although much smaller and less luxurious, proved to be far more comfortable. Sticking strictly to the instructions I had received at King Street, I avoided coming into contact with anyone I took to be English, but a little old lady, sitting on the seat opposite mine, and clutching a large bulging straw basket, recognized that I was not a native. After subjecting me to close scrutiny for some time she could not contain her curiosity any longer.

'You English, you go Spain?' she asked.

'Yes,' I replied, with a nod of my head to remove any ambiguity, and busied myself with peering through the train window to avoid further conversation. Whether this dear old soul was the latest recruit to the French security service I do not know, but she certainly had had little difficulty in recognizing my nationality and my destination. By this time I had become convinced that I was under observation by the French authorities. Since I had landed at Dunkirk I had been aware of a constant police presence: a mackintosh-clad figure over six foot tall and with a pair of size eleven boots seemed to be always in the background, and anyone with a build like that is far from being inconspicuous! But as he did not interfere with me I was quite happy for him to be around; after all, he had his money to earn and doubtless his overtime pay came to quite a tidy sum. Anyway, I reasoned that the French police had nothing to gain by prematurely terminating my journey for since I was in their country without a passport they would have had to send me back to England and this would have put the French tax-payer to an expense which could be avoided by simply allowing me an unhindered passage to Spain.

What I did not learn until recently was that the British police had been keeping a watch on me. Only with the release of the Nottingham Police Committee minutes did I discover that I had been followed by the local constabulary to London and from there by the Metropolitan Police, and other local forces, to Dover. No doubt the English police had alerted the French police to my presence on French soil and this would have accounted for my large watchdog. So the attempts at subterfuge had not been skilful enough to throw either the British or French police off my trail. Changing trains at Arras and Amiens and the lack of contact with my fellow volunteers had been to no avail.

It was a very weary and ill-assorted group of young men who stepped off the train at Perpignan. There seemed to be representatives of any number of European nations stretching cramped limbs and looking to see who was going to set them off on the final stage of their journey over the frontier and into Spain. I was feeling very much the worse for wear. The constant travelling of the last fifty or so hours, the tension and excitement, the lack of sleep or a square meal had begun to take their toll. Food was my most pressing requirement as I had had only a few snacks of French bread and chocolate since landing at Dunkirk. However, we barely had time to glance around the small ill-lit station before we were being speedily assembled by members of the local Communist Party and taken to a hall where a hot meal awaited us. It may appear ungallant but this meal, despite my colossal hunger, was a great disappointment. French peasant

food was much too oily and far too heavily flavoured with garlic for a palate accustomed only to simple English fare. A mug of steaming hot tea would have gone down a treat while the rough red wine served with the meal seemed a very poor second best. Yet it wouldn't be long before I was looking back on that meal at Perpignan with a feeling of nostalgia.

The meal over, we were ushered outside into the chill night and we boarded a darkened bus destined for the Franco-Spanish border. I can recall nothing of the journey between Perpignan and the frontier because the effects of the meal and the wine combined with the warmth of the bus acted like a sleeping draught. I was vaguely aware of a brief conversation between our driver and a frontier guard before the bus lurched forward once again. Some time later the British Government made recruiting for the International Brigades illegal under the Foreign Enlistment Act and put pressure on the French Government to close its border with Spain to stop the flow of recruits making its way south. This created enormous problems but still the volunteers made their way to Spain through the snow-covered mountain passes of the Pyrénées; but I arrived in luxury! I awoke as the bus was covering the last few miles into the Spanish town of Figueras in the opaque light of dawn. Christmas Day, 1936, and I was in Spain.

Our base at Figueras was a magnificent mediaeval fortress which had served as an army post for many years. The regular troops stationed there had not answered the call to insurrection and had opted instead to remain loyal to the Republic. They lost little time in taking us on a conducted tour of the fortress. They proudly showed those of us who were British the grave of an English officer dating from the time of the Peninsular War, but of greatest pride was the dungeon in which their own officers, who had thrown in their lot with Franco, had been cornered and killed. They were most anxious to reaffirm their loyalty to the Republic by taking us to the dungeon in which the rebel officers had made a last stand, before a well-directed hand-grenade had ended their resistance. The blood of those who had died had left dark stains on the whitewash of the shrapnel-pitted walls and served as a foretaste of what lay ahead. It was also in the dungeons at Figueras that many Asturian miners had been imprisoned after their unsuccessful uprising in 1934. (A final act of the Spanish Civil War was to be played out within those same castle walls in February 1939, when the Republic's ministers met there for the last time before fleeing across the border into France and into exile, leaving Spain in the hands of Franco and his co-conspirators.)

It was in the dungeons of Figueras fortress that we were housed, and

despite the dank chill of my new sleeping quarters I felt greatly refreshed when I awoke on a clear and bright Boxing Day morning. We had a few days in Figueras before moving on again and I spent my time wandering round the surrounding town and countryside. There was an air of seasonal festivity in the streets that was totally absent in the castle. Unlike even non-believers back home in England, our military hosts – dedicated Anarchists and Communists – were impervious to the age-old appeal of Christmas, but they were considerate hosts and it was with mixed feelings that I prepared to leave.

It was a magnificent, crisp, sunny morning as we marched raggedly out of the fortress at Figueras and down through the small town to the nearby railway station, and what a send-off the locals gave us! Our shambling appearance and bearing mattered not to them as they thronged the streets to cheer us – as though we were already returning victorious from the front rather than setting off, untrained and untested, to face a force as yet undefeated. A few days' rest, however, had cured the lethargy brought on by the long and tedious journey south and we did our best to convey an impression of strength, confidence and resolution to our warm-hearted admirers.

During our stay at Figueras our numbers had grown as new volunteers poured in from most of the countries of Europe at all hours of the day and night, and it required a special train to take us on the next stage of our journey to Barcelona. The cramped conditions on the train and the soreness wrought by its slatted wooden seats seemed inconsequential when compared to the cheering which greeted the train's arrival at every village halt between Figueras and the capital of Catalonia. This journey was one of the slowest that I have ever experienced by train; whether this was because of a conscious effort to conserve fuel or because the crew was keeping an anxious eye on the track ahead for signs of sabotage, I do not know, but the pace of the train made it possible to jump from it as it passed an orange grove, throw oranges to comrades leaning from the carriage windows and still have time to climb aboard the last coach without having to break into a gallop.

So many people had turned out to watch our stately passage that by the time we reached Barcelona there could not have been a volunteer on that train who doubted that he had made the right decision in coming to Spain; but if there had been any doubt, our reception in Barcelona and the fervour in its streets would have removed the hesitancy in the mind of even the most sceptical. What a city! It was just like a volcano, erupting in all directions at the same time. A breathtaking, awe-inspiring and heart-

warming spectacle of noise, bustle, enthusiasm and gaiety. A revolutionary city in the full flood of revolutionary zest and zeal; an unforgettable sight.

Our welcome to Barcelona began the moment the train pulled into the station. On the platform a band was playing and crowds both inside and outside the station buildings were cheering, singing and shouting political slogans. Against this background of noise and excitement we marched with such military precision as we could muster through the main streets of the city. It seemed as though people from miles around had left their houses, shops, offices and factories to greet us. Every building was festooned with the red flag of the Communists, the red and black of the Anarchists and the colours of the Catalan Nationalists. Every available wall was covered with posters exhorting the people to come to the defence of the Republic and to enter the fight to smash the Fascist insurrectionists. This was indeed a city which belonged to its people, who had taken it into their custody in a series of bloody street skirmishes. All public buildings were occupied by various military groups, of which the Anarchist militia was the most influential: a fact which probably explains why so many of the churches had been desecrated and put to very secular use. Our parade through the main streets of Barcelona ended at the Carlos Marx Barracks which, at the outbreak of the war, had housed an artillery brigade, and which had suffered tremendous damage in a series of protracted battles between its Nationalist defenders and the people's militia before it had finally fallen. No real attempt had been made to restore it to any sort of order: it was in a filthy state and stank to high heaven. Nevertheless, in the midst of the surrounding dirt, and chaos we were fed, before we were paraded back through the vibrating streets to the railway station.

Another slow and tedious journey ensued, this time to Valencia, although the sight of a new land and the unfamiliar smells of a countryside so different from home helped to alleviate the tedium and discomfort of hard seats and snail-like progress.

The joyous reception which we had received in Barcelona could not have been attributed solely to the military potential which we sought to display. Dressed in civilian clothes, and marching as only untrained civilians can march, we could not have conveyed an impression of military might. The warmth of our welcome could only have been explained by our mere presence. The fact that we were volunteers who had come all the way to Spain from many European countries to fight for the Republic's cause must have made the loyal citizens of that country aware that they were not alone in their fight.

In contrast to our welcome in Barcelona was our reception in Valencia. Again, after leaving the train we went on the inevitable, and seemingly mandatory, parade through the streets before devouring the meal which had been prepared for us. However, in Valencia there was no spontaneous excitement; Valencia was not a city which had passed into the control of the people and the Civil War did not seem as immediate as it had done further north.

From Valencia another slow and dreary train journey through the night took us to Albacete which had become the centre for the International Brigades. There we were housed, for what remained of the night, in the former barracks of the Civil Guard. During the uprising of the previous July, the Civil Guard stationed at Albacete had decided to throw in its lot with the Fascists, but had been isolated, as had happened to insurrectionists in many parts of Spain. After several days of being confined to barracks by the presence of the local armed militia their resistance had crumbled and they had been slaughtered. As at Figueras, our triumphant hosts were anxious to show us around the scene of their victory and could not conceal their pride when we were once again called upon to view the blood-splattered walls and floors of the various barrack rooms. Such tours were becoming macabre. It was all quite dreadful and the barracks at Albacete was a horrible place in which to have to sleep.

The following morning after breakfast, we were assembled in the town's bull-ring and paraded in our national groups. Collectively we must have numbered not far short of 600 men. The largest contingents were French and German but the British representation was not small. We in the British contingent were then ordered into open-topped lorries which bounced and swayed along the poorly surfaced Spanish roads for the hour-long journey to Madrigueras, a little village which lay about twenty miles to the north. If Albacete had been lacking in appeal, Madrigueras was little better, especially as it seemed to have an infinite capacity to attract a cold and very dampening drizzle, which enveloped the tedious uniformity of the Plain of La Mancha upon which our new home stood. Like so many Spanish villages I was to see, Madrigueras was characterized by the squalor of its buildings and the almost unbelievable poverty of its peasants: a poverty which struck me most forcibly even though I felt myself to be no stranger to hardship. Compared to the poor peasants of this part of Spain the unemployed of Nottinghamshire were affluent, for Murcia was an area of absentee landlords who gave no thought to the welfare of their tenant workers and were interested only in the profit that they could extract from the land, irrespective of the misery such exploitation caused.

The British base at Madrigueras was already taking shape when I arrived. Wilf McCartney was the Commanding Officer, probably because he had already served in our own armed forces. No doubt Wilf was seen as the man with the experience and qualifications to turn a group of enthusiastic civilians into an effective military unit. Peter Kerrigan was the Political Commissar, a role which he filled with great zest and to good effect. I came to admire Peter, but I was never very impressed with Wilf. Somehow he lacked the aura which I associated with good leaders, he seemed unable to motivate those under him to give of their best, and I was left with the feeling that his abilities as an organizer and decision-maker were rather rudimentary. The problems of knocking us into a fighting unit proved too much for Wilf McCartney.

We were issued with strong boots, rough khaki uniforms, a tin hat of the kind worn at that time by French troops, two coarse woollen blankets and the other accoutrements of a soldier. Thus equipped, at least outwardly we took on a more military appearance. We were also issued with rifles. These were Soviet-made and were identical to those used by the Red Army. They were brand-new and were distributed straight from the packing-cases in which they had come from the Soviet Union. This Soviet rifle was a very good weapon. It was lighter than the Lee Enfield so loved by generations of British infantrymen but equally powerful, and as a result had a considerable recoil. This was its one drawback: when fired by a man wearing only a thin cotton shirt the kick it gave could be quite painful if the correct firing position had not been adopted. No doubt in the Red Army where the troops could be in action in sub-zero temperatures and heavily-clad against the cold, the recoil would hardly be noticeable, but the heat in Spain was such that on many occasions we went into battle naked from the waist up, and after any heavy action there were a lot of sore shoulders. Nevertheless, the rifle was very good-natured and continued to fire under atrocious conditions of heat, flying grit and dust. A drop of oil for the bolt was rarely available, but it still moved freely, and even if the breech became covered in dirt this could be removed by a well-directed bit of huffing and puffing. The fact that no scabbard was issued for the bayonet was more of a problem than the recoil. In the Red Army troops were expected to have the bayonet permanently fixed, but this made the rifle heavier and proved to be a real source of annoyance when crawling through undergrowth or seeking cover in olive groves, as the bayonet kept getting entangled in shrubs and low branches. So most of us took to carrying our bayonets in our belts, and large numbers of them were thus lost. Personally, I always liked to have my bayonet with me and took great

care of it. Although I never had an opportunity to put it to the use for which it was intended, it proved its value on many occasions. Being long, grooved at the sides, and finished with a small, chisel-sharp end, it made an excellent toasting-fork for bread, and was unsurpassed when it came to retrieving baked potatoes from the hot embers of a camp-fire.

The issue of uniforms and rifles generated a fair degree of excitement. I can still remember the sense of pride and power I felt when I first took charge of my brand-new and beautifully greased rifle. I was going to conquer the world with it and nothing and no one was going to stand in my way. So much for the idealism of the soldier who had yet to taste combat!

No doubt to develop a sense of unity among us our battalion was given a name: the Saklatvala Battalion. Shapurji Saklatvala had been a member of parliament for North Battersea, and he enjoyed something of a reputation as a leading light in the Indian Nationalist movement and as a radical politician. Maybe also it was hoped that by using his name some Asian comrades might want to join us, but I never saw any evidence to suggest that this was successful. The name never caught on and was eventually dropped. We became widely known as the British Battalion, *Batallón Inglés*, and were numbered XVI Battalion, XV Brigade, 35th Division of the Spanish Republican Army. Shortly before leaving Madrigueras we were issued with a little metal tab to attach to our jacket collars to identify us. Even the title XVI Battalion did not last for long and we became the 57th and remained so throughout the rest of the war; but we were invariably referred to as 'The British'.

The Battalion comprised three infantry companies, each of around 100 men, and a machine-gun company. Each company was under the command of a lieutenant (*teniente*) and a political commissar (*commissario*). Each company was divided into three sections, each of which was in turn subdivided into three platoons of eight or more men. A section was commanded by a sergeant and a platoon by a corporal. As no one was issued with any badge of rank by which he could be clearly distinguished you had to know by sight who was a sergeant, corporal, etc. so that you would be in a position to know which commands were authoritative and which were less so. The absence of a clearly discernible chain of command did create difficulties and I think that we let ourselves down badly by not having symbols which visibly identified the holders of superior and subordinate positions.

Immediately after surrendering my civilian clothes and receiving my equipment I was assigned to No 3 Company under the command of Lieutenant Bill Briskey. Bill was a quiet, gentle sort of man, a most

unmilitary type to look at but he could be extremely determined and he was most dedicated to the fight against Fascism. Before going to Spain he had been the leader of the busmen's rank-and-file movement in London at the time when the capital's buses were owned and run by a number of different companies. Bill had managed to weld the employees of the disparate companies into one effective trade union organization. Whilst he clearly had a record of service to the working-class movement stretching back over many years, I very much doubt if he had any military knowledge or experience whatsoever. But this was almost a universal problem in the early days of the International Brigades, and one which caused little anxiety, simply because there was nothing practical that could be done to resolve it. The International Brigades had to work with the experience of the men who had enlisted, and if military experience was in short supply that was just too bad. Bill made me his messenger, his *Enlace*, and I was proud and pleased to take on what, in the absence of telephone and radio communications, was a vital task if the company was to function effectively under battle conditions. It was a position I was to keep for a long time and one which meant that I covered many miles on foot, and all too often under enemy fire.

At Madrigueras we were accommodated in the few large houses of the village, which had been owned by Fascist supporters before they had fled to safety elsewhere. By the time we arrived these houses had been stripped clean of their contents and we were obliged to sleep on the floor. This in no way lessened my enthusiasm. At least I was not out in the open, and the two blankets with which I had been issued served to keep the cold of the night at bay. Food was more of a problem. Without going into great detail I think it could be accurately described as awful. We were drawing supplies from the Spanish Quartermaster and naturally it was food native to the region – rice, beans and so on – and we Englishmen were trying to cook it with no real knowledge of the preparation techniques required. Also we had nothing to cook by except open fires made from wood from recently felled trees, which were a devil of a job to kindle. There was also a desperate shortage of water. The water supply for the entire village came from two small fountains, at which there was a constant queue of locals and troops throughout the day and well into the night. Having been accustomed at home to using water as though it was unlimited, it came as something of a shock to find just what a chore it was to obtain the small quantity needed for each day's cooking and washing. If water was in short supply, wine was available in abundance at ridiculously low prices, and there were some initial problems with drunkenness. Another factor which

gave rise to frayed tempers was that it was impossible to obtain tobacco. There was simply nowhere in the village to buy it and we were dependent on what reached us in the parcels from home. As these arrived at irregular intervals we either had a fair quantity of tobacco or none at all. The shortage of tobacco, the shortage of water and the unfamiliar and poorly cooked food probably accounted for the relish with which copious quantities of the local wine were consumed. Wine was never in short supply and was the one redeeming feature of our bleak village.

We got along with the local inhabitants extremely well at all times. Fortunately, a separate canteen for the exclusive use of the Battalion was never set up and so in the evenings we did our drinking in the local bar with the villagers. The bar was, by Spanish tradition, an all-male preserve, and whilst the Anarchists of Madrigueras may have thought that they were well on the way to achieving their revolution some customs are most resistant to change, and no woman was even seen in our 'local'. Often we British drank a drop too much or engaged in that most ill-advised activity of mixing the vino with cognac or anis, with the inevitable outcome. However, we made it a matter of pride to look after our own drunks and our Spanish comrades took our sometimes unruly behaviour good-naturedly. Getting all the drinkers back to their billets after an evening out was a problem on occasions and the streets often echoed to the tune of 'Bandera Rosa', which must have disturbed the more sober citizens who had long since retired to bed. Complaints about our 'boisterous' behaviour were few and far between: a fact which says a great deal about the tolerance and patience of the Spanish people.

At Madrigueras we suddenly discovered that we were going to be paid. No one had ever suggested pay to us and I had not even thought about it. The members of the International Brigades were never called mercenaries and have not been labelled as such even by their worst enemies to this day. Certainly I did not go to Spain for the money, and I cannot believe that anyone else did either, for we were paid at the same rate as the troops of the Spanish Army which at that time was five pesetas a day for an infantryman: an amount which exactly equated with the average daily earnings of a Spanish peasant. As a peseta was worth the equivalent of a British sixpence in 1936, only a fool would have contemplated fighting for such a paltry sum. Surprisingly it proved virtually impossible to spend even this meagre amount. With wine costing but a few centimos a glass we found that we quickly accumulated quite a stack of money in our pockets which we gave to collections for orphans, comforts for the Madrid Fund and other causes connected with the Republic's war effort.

The military training we underwent at Madrigueras may not have matched that experienced by regular troops in the professional armies of the major western European nations but it was far from inadequate. We did a considerable number of route marches to toughen our feet in preparation for the hardships ahead and, as we had a certain amount of ammunition to spare, rifle practice was commonplace. Even though I had fired a rifle before I must have expended fifteen or more rounds on the improvised firing-ranges before moving up to the front. I also had instruction in how to throw a grenade and how to use the folds of the land to gain cover when advancing against enemy positions. I have read accounts in which people claim to have been literally pulled off a train and put into the front line without any form of training whatsoever, but this did not happen to me and it never happened to anyone I have met who fought for the Republic. Given the circumstances in which we found ourselves and the shortage of skilled and experienced military personnel, I think that the training we received was as good as could have been expected. Indeed our training improved after we had been at Madrigueras for a couple of weeks when those of our fellow countrymen who had already seen action on the Córdoba Front were sent to strengthen the newly formed British Battalion. These men were a tremendous asset to us: they came to us with the dust of the battlefield upon them and gave our morale a wonderful boost at a time when our initial enthusiasm for combat-training was just beginning to flag. Their actual experience of combat against the Fascist forces was worth far more than anything we could learn from parade-ground manoeuvres. They epitomized the spirit of the fight against Fascism.

On 6th February, after five weeks of training, Madrigueras burst into activity in a way that it had not done previously. We were ordered to pack our gear and board a fleet of lorries which were waiting to take us to the railway station in Albacete. By nightfall we were in a slow-moving, blacked-out train bound for Villarrubia de Santiago, a few miles east of Aranjuez, and by early the next morning we were marching into the small, miserable, poverty-stricken village of Chinchón which overlooks the valley of the Tajuna. On the far side of the valley rose the hills of the Sierra Pingarrón from which came the distant rumble of artillery and later, as night drew in, the flashes of the heavy guns could be seen. My first battle now lay just ahead.

* * *

Anti-Fascist fervour in Britain was not confined to the containment of Oswald Mosley's blackshirts. The outbreak of the Spanish Civil War, in July 1936, was the subject of intense debate. Although few really understood the complexities of Spanish society and the tensions which led to the outbreak of hostilities, there was widespread opposition to the attempt by the Spanish Army to seize power from the largely liberal dominated government. The fact that the government had been democratically elected by a broad coalition of left-wing political parties under the banner of a Popular Front, whereas the rebels appeared, to represent the traditional élites in Spanish society – the Army, the Church and the aristocracy – was sufficient to inflame public opinion in Britain. In the following months, evidence that Franco's Army of Africa had been transported to the Spanish mainland by German military aircraft, and that the rebels had accepted both men and arms from Germany and Italy, further fuelled the conviction that Spain was being subjected to a Fascist coup.

From the outset, however, the British government adopted a position of strict neutrality, banning the export of war material to Spain in August 1936 and participating as a founder member in the international Non-Intervention Committee established in the following month. This position was underlined in the opening months of 1937 when, with the invoking of the Foreign Enlistment Act, the despatch of volunteers to fight in Spain was formally prohibited. It was apparent that, despite extensive evidence that non-intervention was little more than a façade and that Spain was developing into an international battlefield, with Germany and Italy supplying the rebel forces with men and war materials and the Soviet Union providing assistance to the Republican Government, the British Government was determined to avoid involvement in the Spanish imbroglio. It would seem that the Baldwin government was not willing to risk the escalation of the Spanish conflict into a full-blown confrontation with Germany and Italy at a time when the appeasement of the dictators was still the central goal of British foreign policy. If the British government was unwilling to assist the Republican government they could not, though, stem the tide of popular support for the Republican cause. With the establishment of the National Joint Committee for Spanish Relief and the proliferation of local Aid Spain organizations, vast amounts of money were raised to ship supplies of food and clothing to the

Republican government. Although elements of the trade union movement threw themselves actively into the fund-raising campaign, the Labour Party remained curiously divided and muted. Certainly the party declared its support for the Republican cause in principle and condemned breaches of the Non-Intervention agreement but it was wary of committing itself to a demand for military assistance to the Republic, and was innately suspicious of the linkages between the Republic and the Soviet Union. The Communist Party, however, had no such inhibitions and from the outset declared itself wholeheartedly for the Republic. While the other political parties hesitated, the Communist Party took the initiative in recruiting volunteers to fight for the Republic.

Although the recruitment of volunteers was formally prohibited by the British government in February 1937, the Communist Party continued to despatch men to Spain throughout the conflict and well over 2,000 Britons fought for the Republic in the period 1936–1939. The first batch of volunteers arrived in Spain in October and November of 1936 and, with little or no training and equipped with a variety of uniforms and weapons, they were rushed to take part in the defence of Madrid. A further group of Britons fought on the Córdoba Front in southern Spain but the first recognizable British unit did not emerge until December 1936 as No 1 Company of the Franco-Belgian Battalion of the XIV (Marseillaise) International Brigade.

This unit was engaged in heavy fighting north of Madrid in the last week of December as the Republican Army sought to prevent the Nationalists severing Madrid's lines of communication with northern Spain. The British unit was formally disbanded the following month when the decision was taken to form a purely British Battalion attached to the XV Brigade. Therefore, after December 1936 all British volunteers upon arrival at the International Brigade headquarters in Albacete were despatched to Madrigueras where the British Battalion was based.

Although the International Brigades were largely associated with the various European Communist Parties and indeed were formed as a result of an initiative by the Moscow-based Communist International, only approximately half of the British volunteers were actually Communist Party members. They were very much a mixed bag which contained a smattering of middle-class intellectuals and a large number of working-class men, generally drawn

from the regions which had endured the highest levels of unemployment. Few had military experience of any sort and while some travelled to Spain purely out of a sense of adventure, they were bound together in most instances by their experiences of the Depression and the common cause of anti-Fascism. In this context the decision to join the International Brigade was a continuation of the fight against privilege and injustice which gave a meaning and purpose to their lives. Undoubtedly the majority were men of courage but they were to pay a high price for their principles in that as many as one in four of those who left for Spain was to give his life for the Republican cause.

The first shots of the Spanish Civil War had been fired on the evening of 17th July 1936 as officers and men of the Foreign Legion in Spanish Morocco seized key government buildings in Tetian and Ceuta. This action was part of a carefully orchestrated plot involving officers of the Army and the Civil Guard throughout Spain. In the following week under the direction of General Mola, who had directed the uprising from Pamplona, rebel officers seized control of most of the provinces of Navarre, Old Castile, Galicia and Aragon. This enclave in northern Spain was soon supplemented by General Gonzalo Queipo de Llano who, from his base in Seville, delivered much of Andalusia to the rebel cause, including the key port of Cadiz. In their attempt to oust the civilian government which the generals claimed was exposing the nation to the threat of Communist insurrection, it was anticipated that the rebels would receive the sympathy of the Church, the middle classes and the landed interest, plus the active support of the armed forces and several paramilitary right-wing political units such as the Carlists and the Falange. The events of the opening week of the rebellion, however, were not entirely auspicious for General Mola and his supporters for, although the rebels controlled approximately one-third of Spain, most of the Spanish Navy, the Air Force and in many areas the Civil Guard remained loyal to the Republican government. Furthermore, in the major industrial cities the uprising was met initially by a General Strike and within days by a broad coalition of left-wing political parties and trade unions. In both Madrid and Barcelona the rebel forces quickly found themselves besieged within their barracks and were faced with the prospect of either surrender or death at the hands of

a force of loyal officers, civil guard and armed workers. Yet from this opening the rebels, or as they later styled themselves, the Nationalists, were soon to consolidate and expand their control over vast tracts of Spain. A key element of their success was undoubtedly the high level of military expertise within their ranks which allowed them to supplement their reservoir of regular troops with raw recruits and conscripts who could be welded quickly and efficiently into formidable fighting units. In comparison, the Republican forces, although not lacking in numbers or commitment, were disorganized and as often preoccupied with internal feuding as with the task of defeating the enemy. The strength of the Republic lay in its ability to draw upon a wide spectrum of political support, ranging from liberal centre parties to the more extreme left-wing Communist and Anarchist factions to oppose the Army coup. In military terms, however, this strength was ironically a source of weakness, for many of the political factions jealously guarded their independence and insisted upon forming independent military formations. The problem of attempting to establish any sort of military discipline or command structure amongst the various factions, some of which seemed far more concerned with engineering a social revolution than simply defeating the Nationalists, was a factor which was to plague the Republic throughout the war.

In the early days of the war the Republicans often made up for what they lacked in military organization with sheer weight of numbers and fanatical fervour. With support from sections of the armed forces and the civil guard and armed with a motley array of weapons, generally seized from captured Army barracks, they enjoyed remarkable success, largely due to the support of the urban working-class and in some regions the peasantry who saw in the rebellion the hand of the traditional ruling élites. Within a month, however, the balance of power had shifted dramatically towards the Nationalist forces. The determining factor was almost certainly the discrepancy in the foreign military assistance provided to the Republican and Nationalist armies. Whether through fear of Communism or perhaps simply as a means of expanding their influence in the western Mediterranean, within days of the opening of hostilities Italy and Germany were despatching extensive military aid to the Nationalist forces. The provision of fuel, guns, tank, aircraft and trained personnel to man the equipment

gave the Nationalists a superiority that Soviet aid to the Republic was never quite able to match. Mussolini also provided up to 47,000 troops to boost the Nationalist Army while Italian submarines carried out a series of attacks on merchant shipping supplying the Republic. Furthermore, although the two Nationalist enclaves appeared geographically isolated, assistance from the Portuguese government allowed them to maintain lines of communication and supply both with each other and with their new-found allies.

It appeared, therefore, that from the outset, while the origins of the war were very much tied up with the complexities of Spanish society, the course of the military confrontation was heavily influenced by the provision of foreign military assistance which led

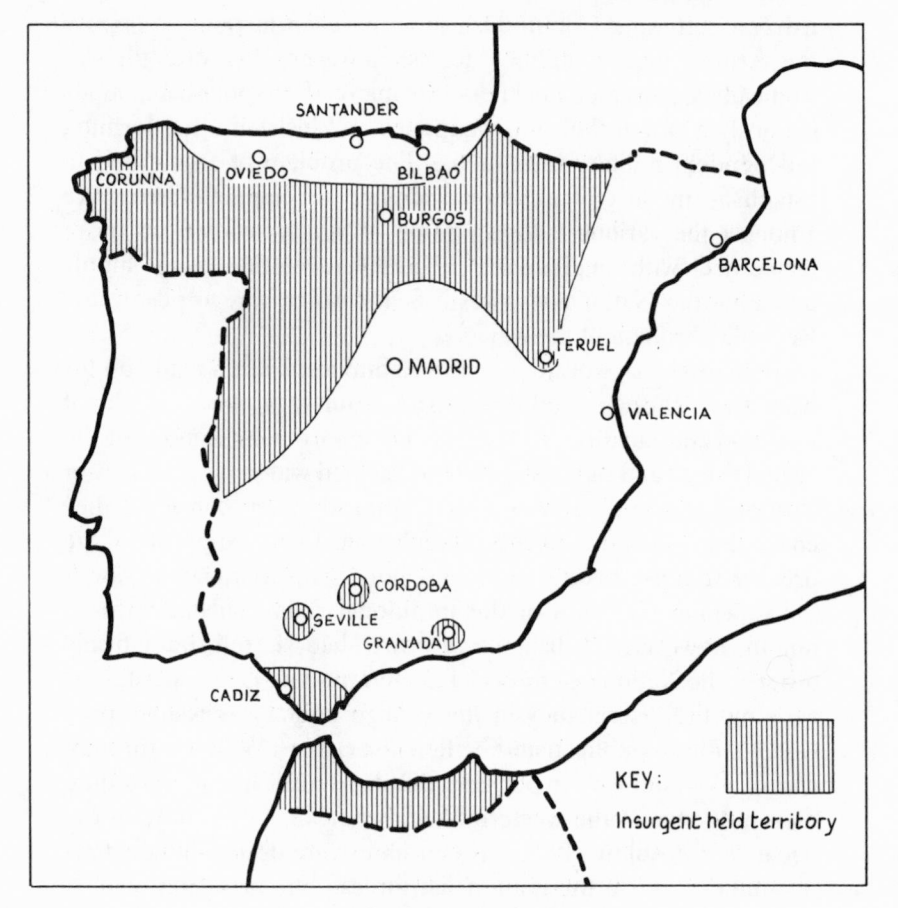

Spain July 1936

to the suggestion that Spain was rapidly turned into an international battlefield. Certainly, without the loan of twenty Junkers 52 aircraft from Germany Franco would have encountered great difficulty in transporting the Army of Africa from Morocco to the Spanish mainland where it was to play such a decisive role in the opening months of the war. It was the arrival of Franco and his mixed force of foreign legionnaires and Moors which effectively swung the balance of forces in southern Spain in the Nationalists' favour and, in the months of August and September, they steadily fought their way northwards through Extremadura routing the Republican garrisons at Badajoz, Merida and Talavera and relieving the siege of the Alcazar in the last week of September. By October Franco had linked up with General Mola's forces uniting the two Nationalist enclaves and now within striking distance of Madrid.

In October 1936 Madrid typified the problems confronting the Republic. There was no shortage of volunteers to defend the capital and its citizens were prepared to work day and night to construct fortifications to defend the western approaches to the city. Yet, due to bickering and feuding, the defence of Madrid was in a precarious situation. By the first week of November, as the Nationalist forces began to converge on the city, the government, anticipating the fall of the capital, moved to Valencia. As it turned out this was a fortuitous decision for with the departure of the government much of the previous political intrigue was removed, and the new military commander, General Miaja, capitalizing on stories of atrocities perpetrated by Franco's Moors against Republican soldiers and sympathizers, was finally able to weld his units into a coherent and determined fighting unit. Over a period of almost a month the Republicans, assisted by the arrival of Soviet tanks and aircraft, met and held the Nationalist advance in a series of prolonged and fierce battles to the west of Madrid. This victory was a tribute to the heroism of the people of Madrid and the growing professionalism of the Republican army but was also assisted by the introduction of the International Brigades into the conflict. The XIth Brigade consisting of three battalions of Germans, Poles, Hungarians and Yugoslavs had been formed as recently as 22nd October 1936 and armed with a startling variety of weapons it was thrown into the front line west of Madrid on 8th November.

It was followed five days later by the XIIth Brigade made up of Italian and French volunteers. The military impact of these hastily assembled brigades is difficult to assess although certainly their appearance served to raise the morale of the Republican units and the XIth Brigade played a significant part in the decisive battle for the University City on 15th and 16th November which contributed to the Nationalists' decision to abandon frontal assaults on the capital.

If, by 18th November, the initial battle for Madrid appeared to have been won, in reality this merely marked the conclusion of the first phase of the siege of Madrid. The control of the capital, although of little strategic value, was seen by both sides as of vital psychological importance.

2

The Battle of Jarama

In the winter of 1936–7, the Nationalist forces abandoned their assault on the western approaches to Madrid and sought to encircle it. Their first thrust was to the north of the city but, following a series of offensives over a period of five weeks, they only succeeded in cutting the highway to Corunna which ran north-west from Madrid. By the second week of January 1937 it was evident that their attack had effectively ground to a halt. One of the factors inhibiting their advance was the unsuitability of the terrain for their German and Italian tank units. The terrain to the south of the capital, however, appeared far more inviting. By mid-January General Orgaz had assembled 40,000 Nationalist soldiers for an assault designed to sweep across the valley of the Jarama river and eventually cut the Madrid-Valencia highway running south-east out of the capital. If the attack were to succeed it would leave Madrid's lines of communication and supply perilously exposed and effectively outflank the defensive positions established west of the capital.

At his disposal Orgaz had the battle-hardened Army of Africa whose foreign legionnaires and Moors had established a reputation for unbridled brutality as they had fought their way north from Seville. The force was divided into five columns each equipped with an impressive array of artillery, heavy machine-guns and anti-tank guns. In addition Orgaz was able to call upon the support of two German tank companies and the air power of the German Condor Legion. The attack opened on 6th February and in the first five days met with initial success in sweeping east to the Jarama valley, but the advance was slower than anticipated as the Nationalists encountered Republican troops who had also been massing for an offensive south of Madrid. Furthermore, the introduction of Soviet tanks and aircraft gave the Republic a

superiority in firepower that was to be repeated only rarely in the
following two years. On 11th February, however, the Nationalists
managed to cross the Jarama in force in two places and it was
apparent that if they succeeded in taking the heights to the east of
the river a major breakthrough was within their grasp. At this point
the Republic threw in its reserves, including three International
Brigades. The now battle-hardened XIth and XIIth Brigades were
committed to the north where the Nationalists had made most
inroads. The newly formed XVth Brigade, containing the British
Battalion, was despatched to the south where the Nationalists had
crossed the river at San Martin de la Vega and were advancing on
the heights of Pingarrón. Of the 600 of the British Battalion a

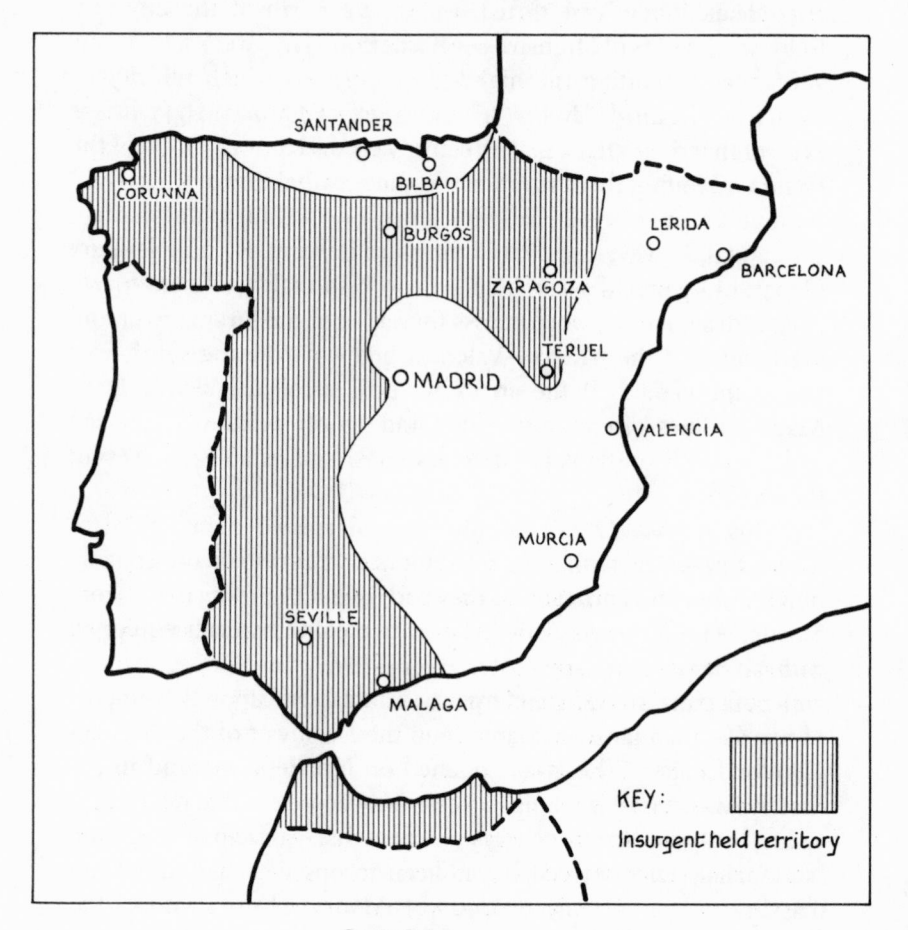

Spain January 1937

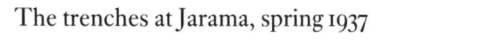

The British Battalion on parade before the Battle of Jarama

The trenches at Jarama, spring 1937

Above: Sierra Pingarrón, 1981. This was the position held by the British Battalion at the Battle of Jarama in February 1937. The Fascists held the Knoll behind Walter. Suicide Valley is in the centre. On the extreme left was the British Battalion's machine-guns' position. In the far background is the hill which was held by the British on the first day of the battle.

Below: A grave of the British dead at the Battle of Jarama

La Pasionaria Hospital, Murcia, February 1937. Walter, in the centre of the back row, with Jewish comrades from London and New York. The building in the background is a former bishop's palace.

Top left: General José Miaja, who took command of the Battle of Jarama and was the foremost Republican general right through the war

Top right: Major R.H. Merriman, Chief of Staff, XV Brigade

Left: Vladimir Ćopić, Commander of the XV Brigade

handful had fought in the battle for the Corunna Road but, for the majority, who had only recently arrived in Spain and had been hastily trained and equipped at Madrigueras, it was to be their first taste of battle and few had any conception of what lay ahead.

* * *

I had expected to go into action within a day of arriving at Chinchón, but that was not to be. It seemed that the British Battalion was to be held in reserve until the pattern of the attack had developed and the Republican commanders had a clear idea of where any major breakthrough was likely to occur. Fortunately, the initial Fascist thrust had been met and held by troops who were already in the area waiting for a Republican offensive to the south of Madrid which would have prevented its encirclement. It was those troops who took the full force of the Fascist attack. I dread to think what would have happened had they not been there or what would have been the outcome had we not already been making our way to the front when the attack developed. I feel sure that Madrid would have been encircled and quickly fallen into Fascist hands. The effect of such an outcome on Republican morale would have been catastrophic. As it was, the big, ugly iron bridge at Arganda came under prolonged and heavy enemy artillery fire, but the road between Madrid and Valencia was kept open.

While the guns thundered and the two opposing air forces fought a number of spectacular dog fights in the clear blue skies above, the British Battalion sought to make itself as comfortable as possible in Chinchón: a task that was far from easy as the village was a filthy little dump with nothing to commend it. It had enjoyed a brief notoriety before the Insurrection when the local priest, acting on his own initiative, had tossed a hand-grenade into a crowded Anarchist meeting with impressive, if gruesome, results. Further back in its history another priest of Chinchón had gained some fame through his family connection with Goya, the world famous artist. The squalor of Chinchón was not, however, in any way alleviated by such past glories.

On the night of 11th February the tension of waiting to go into action, which was beginning to jar the nerve-endings of even the most stoical of my comrades, was ended when without warning we were abruptly ordered to board a fleet of lorries which took us across the Tajuna Valley to the outskirts of Morata de Tajuna, a large village in the foothills of the Sierra Pingarrón. Before dawn broke we were served copious quantities of

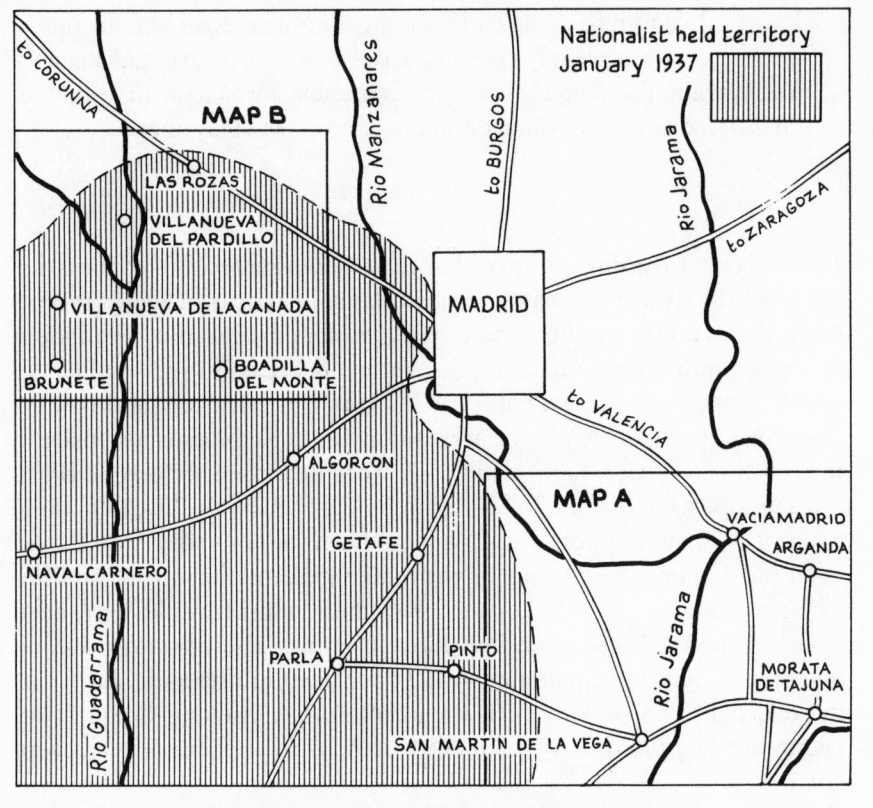

The Battle for Madrid January to July 1937
(See p. 46 for Map A and p. 68 for Map B.)

coffee and as the sun rose we began the march up the hillsides which
overlooked the village, each Company in single file.

There was a calm in the ranks for we had been told that we were to take
up a reserve position behind the front line which had been established on
the east bank of the River Jarama. As we approached the plateau top of the
hills we were met by a breathless messenger who, much to our surprise,
informed us that there was no longer a front line ahead, for a Fascist
offensive which had been launched under cover of darkness had broken
our front and was still maintaining its momentum. Our marching columns
were dispersed with all speed and we spread out into battle formation with
No 3 Company on the left flank of the Battalion. We removed and stacked
our packs and any other equipment which was considered to be
superfluous to our immediate needs and continued with the final part of
the uphill march. The fact that we left equipment behind us testifies to

44

our feelings of confidence, for we were certain that it would not be long before we would be walking back down the hillside to collect it when we had sorted out the minor difficulty which the Fascist advance and the collapse of our front-line had occasioned. Such optimism! Yet, the beauty of a crisp, sunlit, early spring morning and the total absence of any artillery barrage or aerial bombardment gave no indication of the ferocity of the fighting which was now only a very short time away.

There was no hint of panic and no sign of disorder as we took up our positions. All of the training we had undergone at Madrigueras paid off handsomely with everyone perfectly clear of his position and duty. We looked magnificent, we felt magnificent, and we thought that if only our colleagues back home who had made it possible for us to be there could see us now, how proud they would be that we had started to repay them for their efforts with such an impressive display of military style.

When we finally came over the crest of the Sierra Pingarrón, No 4 Company was despatched to occupy a hill to our right, called Casa Blanca Hill after the white farmhouse which stood on its slopes. No 1 Company took a hill to the north side of Casa Blanca Hill, Conical Hill. These two companies had barely had time to establish themselves on their respective summits than they came under attack from the Fascists who were obviously intent on securing such strategically valuable positions for themselves. Meanwhile, No 3 Company was ploughing its way through an olive grove to a spot from which it was possible to look right down the valley through which the River Jarama flowed and toward the distant Pindoque Bridge. Even from a distance we could clearly see Fascist troops in their hundreds pouring over a nearer bridge which had fallen into their hands in a surprise raid a few nights before.

Realizing the virtual impossibility of taking Casa Blanca Hill in the face of determined resistance from Nos 1 and 4 Companies, the Fascist troops pulled back and summoned artillery support. An intense barrage began to fall on the hill, with the white farm buildings no doubt providing an ideal guide for the gunners. In no time at all the buildings which had been a prominent feature of the landscape were reduced to nothing but smoking rubble. Still shells were poured on to Casa Blanca Hill for hour after hour, throwing clouds of dust upward to hang heavily in the still air. The odd stray shell fell toward No 3 Company but we were far enough away from the centre of the action to escape any serious attention or damage. Indeed we were almost reduced to the role of spectators. Bill Briskey decided to ask for instructions from Battalion Headquarters to see if we should be bolstering Nos 1 and 4 Companies who were taking such a fearful

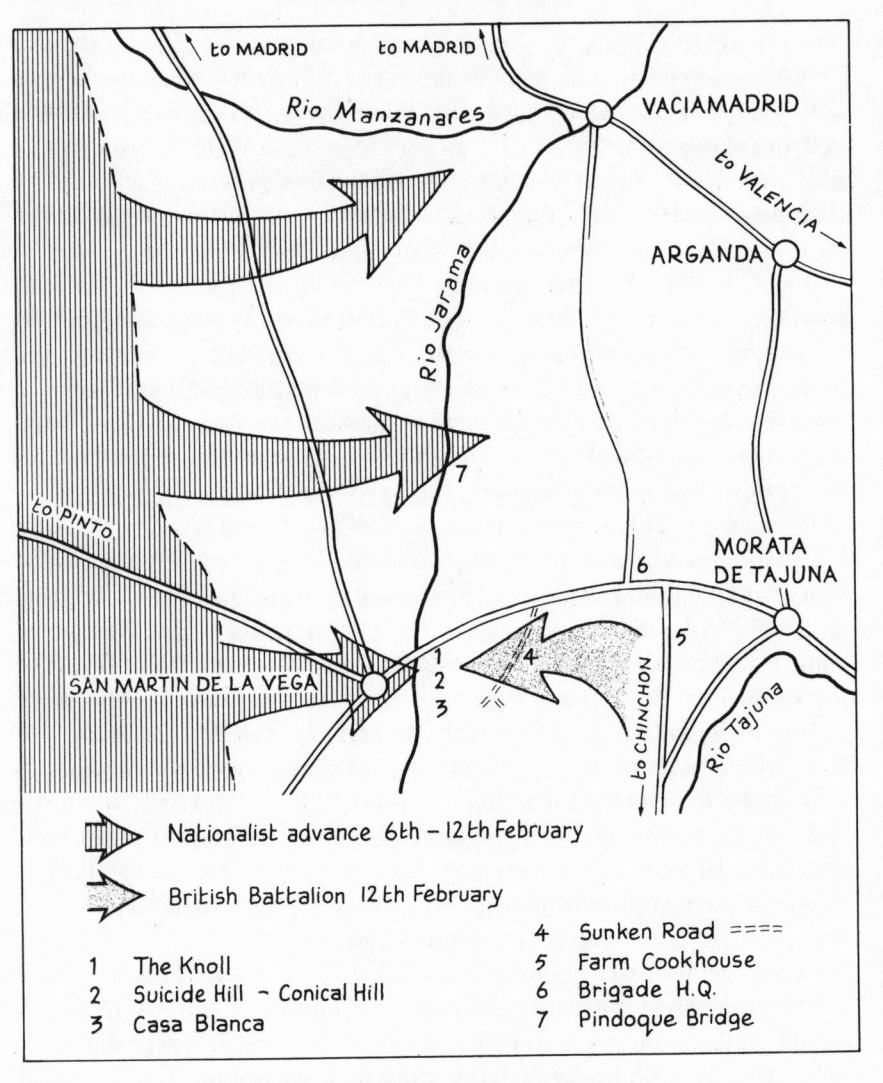

Map A: The Battle of Jarama – Engagement of
the British Battalion 12th February 1937

pounding. As Bill's *Enlace* it was up to me to carry his message to the
Commanding Officer and bring back his instructions to the Company. I
set off, running across the valley floor as though I was competing in the
final of the 100 metres at an Olympic Games. Shells were dropping all
around me and I weaved about in the hope of gaining added protection.
Occasionally, to recover my breath or when a shell exploded a little too

close for comfort, I would throw myself on the ground to get whatever cover was available. The intensity of the shelling, however, soon made me realize that any delay could prove fatal, and that my best chance of survival lay in getting across the more exposed parts of the valley floor and to the relative safety of Battalion Headquarters with all speed.

Seeking protection from the barrage by using the folds of the land meant that I had to pass the leeside of Casa Blanca Hill itself, and when I reached there the carnage was horrendous. There were not only dead and dreadfully wounded men lying all over the ground but there were bits of bodies thrown all over the hillside. If there is anything worse than seeing a dead or horribly wounded man it is seeing just an arm or a leg ripped off and flung aside by the explosion of a shell. I reached Battalion Headquarters without so much as a scratch, and delivered Bill's message. I was told that support from No 3 Company was not needed, and that a retreat had been ordered. I can still remember the instructions I was given to carry back to Bill: 'We have to retreat. No 3 Company is to fall back in good order and keep in line with us.'

I now had to recross the valley floor back to No 3 Company and, as the shelling showed no signs of having abated, I was less than enthusiastic about my chances of lasting long enough to relay the message to Bill. Still I was the company's *Enlace* and *Enlaces* carry instructions and I had been given mine, so off I set at the same furious pace with which I had come. Suddenly the shelling stopped and I stopped running. What was happening? The answer came immediately. Pouring down from the top of Casa Blanca Hill, shrieking loud enough to awaken the dead, came score upon score of Moorish soldiers from the Army of Africa which had been brought over to the Spanish mainland, in aeroplanes furnished by Germany, at the start of the Insurrection. Now they were coming straight toward me, yelling their battle cries to terrify their enemies and to bolster their own courage. They certainly succeeded in terrifying me! In a matter of seconds they seemed to be all around me, but just to my right appeared what I am prepared to swear was the biggest Moor who had ever been born: a huge fellow with a full beard, dressed in a flowing poncho and sporting a fancy line in turbans. He seemed unaware of my presence and was gazing intently toward his left and at whatever was happening beyond my right shoulder where the Battalion was falling back up the valley. He was holding his rifle at arm's length, parallel to the ground, so I brought up my own rifle, lined him up in my sights, and fired. I felt the recoil of the rifle against my shoulder but the Moor remained standing as before. I cursed myself for being such an incompetent fool. The biggest Moor in

the Army of Africa was standing within yards of me and I, armed with a rifle and with an unrestricted field of fire, had somehow contrived to shoot wide of the target! Incredulously, and with a mounting feeling of panic, I hastily reloaded and again took aim. Before I could pull the trigger for a second time my enormous Moor sank slowly to the ground as though he was an inflatable model which had suddenly developed a major leak. As he lay there in the dust he looked for all the world like a pile of washing ready to go into the tub on a Monday morning. There was no time in the heat of the moment to feel either triumph or remorse; it was enough that I was still alive and my only thought was to find Bill Briskey.

Again I set off toward where I had left No 3 Company but, even as I did so, I could see them falling back through the olive grove which we had crossed earlier in the day. Where the Company had been when I left it there were now enemy troops in considerable strength. I was surprised to see some little way in front of me Bill Briskey charging across the exposed ground clearly intent on reaching me. Why Bill tried to meet me I shall never know for when we were separated by but a few yards he suddenly doubled up and wrapped his arms around his chest before pitching forward. In seconds I was bending over him but he was already dead. I have often since speculated on why Bill left the relative safety of the olive grove to cross the exposed valley floor to reach me. Bill was a very kindly, caring sort of fellow and perhaps he thought that I could not see that the position the Company had held when he had despatched me to Battalion Headquarters had fallen into enemy hands and perhaps he was trying to warn me lest I blundered into the Moorish troops. On the other hand, Bill was extremely conscientious and it could have been that he was troubled by having given the Company the order to retreat without having received instructions to do so and was alarmed at having taken such a major decision on his own initiative. If this was the case poor Bill never learnt that he had already done what was expected of him. Whatever the reasons for his action, Bill certainly lost his life in the attempt to meet me.

But on that first day at Jarama, there was no time for thinking, only for action. Even as I bent over Bill's prostrate body I heard a shout behind me. Another Moor was coming toward me and like his recently deceased comrade he also seemed to be a fine specimen of Arabic manhood. The heat of the battle, anger and outrage at Bill's death, and the closeness of the enemy made me think that hand-to-hand combat was now the order of the day and I prepared to meet my new adversary with my bayonet. Of course he was an experienced fighter and I was just a green mug. He had no thoughts of hand-to-hand confrontation in his head. When he was

about twenty feet from me he just pulled, the trigger of his rifle as I should have done if I had had any sense. Fortunately for me, his bullet hit the metal work of my rifle and the smashed and ricocheting bullet took the thumb knuckle of my right hand away. The impact spun me round and I fell to the ground in a dead faint. My luck must have been in that day, for the Moor did not put another round into me, or give me a poke with his bayonet to make sure I was done for.

I must have been unconscious for some time, because when I came back into the world of the living I found that I was now in no-man's-land, for the Battalion had fallen back to a sunken road to my left, and established a defensive line along its length, while the Moors had pulled back to the safety of the hill tops to my right. Grasping my rifle in my left hand, I began to crawl through the bodies of the dead and dying British and Moorish troops intent on reaching the Battalion's new position. Caught in the cross-fire between the opposing troops I did not dare raise myself above the ground and clutching the Soviet-made rifle, of which I had been so proud at Madrigueras but which was now in a filthy condition, I began crawling from the battlefield. My rifle still had a round slammed up the breech and the safety mechanism was in the 'off' position, but I doubt if I would have been able to use it effectively with one hand, and certainly I could not have reloaded had the need arisen. I did not have to crawl far before the land dipped away, covering me from the enemy's view, and I was able to stand upright and move easily and quickly to safety. Bullets still flew above my head every inch of the way but no longer did they contain any real menace as I worked my way toward the rear of our forces. Here I had another piece of good fortune, for I met a soldier from a Spanish Battalion who was in possession not only of a full water-bottle but who also had a good supply of bandages. Whether he came from a unit which had occupied the original front line, which had fallen to the Fascist forces the night before, or whether he came from a newly committed reserve battalion I never knew, but he quickly and skilfully strapped my damaged thumb, from which the knuckle was protruding, and gave me a drink from his canteen. Expecting to find the canteen full of water I took a good long pull at it, only to find myself with a burning throat and coughing fit, for my new-found friend had filled his water-bottle with raw wood alcohol, which, I have to admit, probably pulled me round far faster than a mouthful of water could ever have done.

Having examined my damaged thumb before it was bandaged, having felt the pain that seemed to grow as time went by, and having tried, and failed, to grasp my rifle in my right hand, I had to accept that my career as a

front-line soldier had come to an abrupt end for the near future. There was nothing else for it but to make my way back toward the dressing-station which was situated well to the rear of our position. Some distance from the front a passing ambulance gave me a lift for the remainder of the journey to the dressing-station, which presented an awful sight. There were wounded troops lying all over the place with more arriving all the time. There was a shortage of doctors, nurses and medical supplies and even the most gravely wounded simply had to be left lying in the open air until they could be attended to. Compared to most I saw at the dressing-station I would have qualified as A1 for immediate military service. I waited all night there before a doctor could look at my thumb and during the course of the next day Tommy Wintringham, the Commander of the British Battalion, was brought in on a stretcher, having been wounded in the leg while defending the sunken road. Tommy's spell in charge of the Battalion had been brief. He had replaced Wilf McCartney as Commander when Wilf had been accidentally wounded in the foot by a round from a pistol just before the Battalion left Madrigueras for the front. Wilf's wound had proved to be sufficiently serious for him to be sent home to England for further treatment. How Wilf would have performed under battle conditions remained an unanswered question, but Tommy enjoyed popularity among his men and also possessed a real appreciation of military tactics: he was a fine officer. As Tommy lay on his stretcher awaiting surgery I remember asking him:

'What was the name of that battle, Tommy?'

'Well,' he replied, 'it was fought at a village called Morata de Tajuna, so no doubt that is what they'll call it.'

Later events proved Tommy wrong, as the battle has become universally known as the Battle of Jarama, after the valley along which it was fought.

The first day of that battle brought home to me, and I am sure to many others, the problems that the International Brigades faced in coping with their casualties. Although the medical staff we had were excellent, they were too few and they were not sufficiently well-equipped to handle many of the operations needed for the grievously wounded men. For example, when the British Battalion went into action for the first time we had a battalion doctor, an ambulance which belonged to the battalion and which ferried our own wounded to the dressing-station and operated a shuttle service between the front line and the dressing-station, and four or five stretcher-bearers assigned to the battalion. Two problems immediately became obvious. First, the distance from the front line to the dressing-

station was about four or five kilometres – a long way for even a superficially wounded man to travel under his own steam. Secondly, four or five stretcher-bearers, not per company, but for a battalion of 600 men engaged in heavy fighting, were far too few. Although this appears to be a fearful picture, and although men most certainly died outside the dressing-station while awaiting attention, wounded men at the front would still have had to be dragged to safety by their fellow soldiers, no matter how many stretcher-bearers were available. The expectation of being carried from the front, under fire, and on a stretcher, is totally unrealistic. At Jarama, battalion headquarters served as an assembly- point for the wounded and they waited there for the ambulance to collect them and transport them to the dressing-station. Here another problem arose, and indeed remained throughout the Spanish Civil War, namely that Republican ambulances were invariably subjected to Fascist artillery fire. The Geneva Convention and the Red Cross were simply ignored by the Fascists, and a number of our doctors were killed while tending the wounded. I only hope that our side acted with more humanity, but, at the time, not being in the artillery I never knew, and if I am honest I must admit that I never troubled to find out. Under the circumstances in which we fought, the severely wounded exhibited remarkable fortitude, and the doctors, few of whom were British but who came primarily from Canada and the United States, performed miracles. I cannot speak too highly of them.

The Battle of Jarama was a long drawn-out affair, but it never subsequently reached the level of ferocity which it had attained on its first day. The British Battalion took a frightful battering. We had gone into action without any aerial cover and with no artillery to support us. Despite this Jarama was a triumph for the Republican cause. The sacrifices made on 12th February 1937 by men with relatively little military training and an almost total dearth of combat experience, proved up to the task of withholding the Fascist offensive. War is far too horrible to glorify and romanticize, but I shall never forget the heroism that men fighting for the cause of liberty and justice, in a land that was not their own, exhibited that day. They paid a heavy price for their bravery but Madrid was saved and the Republic lived to fight again.

That first day established the pattern for the weeks of toil and agony which lay ahead at Jarama. It had been a day which had been finely balanced and perhaps hinged around the British Battalion's machine-gun company. When initially called upon to act in support of the Battalion's infantry companies, the machine-gun company had been unable to do so. Because of one of those ironic twists of fate which seem so often to

determine the outcome of battles, and perhaps even of wars, the machine-gunners had been provided with belts of ammunition which did not fit their guns. This meant that the correct ammunition had to be brought to them, the wrong ammunition manually removed from the belts, and the belts reloaded with bullets of the appropriate calibre. Under any conditions this is a lengthy and laborious task; under battle conditions it assumes almost insurmountable proportions. The machine-gunners did, however, accomplish it but not until late in the afternoon, and not a minute before time. The Moors, having seen us fall back, occupied our initial positions and, meeting with only sporadic and rather uncoordinated rifle fire, regrouped and decided that they could continue their advance with little fear of meeting serious and concerted resistance. However, when they attempted to do so they encountered the full blast of the freshly reloaded machine-guns which, although still restricted in ammunition, were sufficiently well-directed to take a heavy toll of the attackers, who were forced to abandon any further thoughts of advance. Jarama thus settled into a pattern of two opposing front lines, and like trench warfare of the First World War, each side sought to feel out the other's weaknesses in the hope of gaining the ascendancy. By the time the fighting reached that stage I was long gone and quite a distance removed from Jarama.

Within a few hours of receiving medical treatment for my thumb I was on board the inevitably slow-moving train travelling away from the front. The walking wounded, myself included, were in a conventional coach, but most of the train had been converted to take more seriously injured stretcher-cases. Medical staff accompanied the train but were far too busy tending the badly wounded to have any time for those still capable of fending for themselves. Food was also available, which was just as well, since it took a little over twenty-four hours before we trundled down the fertile valley which led into the town of Murcia.

At the railway station we were met by a fleet of cars and a variety of other vehicles which bore all the signs of having been hastily commandeered as ambulances to take the stretcher-cases to nearby hospitals. Those of us who were capable of walking were placed in the charge of a railway official who took us through the town to a hospital on the outskirts: a huge place, standing next to what had been the local bishop's palace. The hospital itself had been a convent before the outbreak of hostilities, and had been renamed La Pasionaria Hospital after the charismatic Communist leader, Dolores Ibarruri. Despite its size, the train-load of wounded from the first day of fighting at Jarama filled every available space in the improvised medical centre. Most of the nuns had left, but some of them who had a

knowledge of nursing had stayed behind, and were now offering their valuable services to the small medical team there. As at the front, medical staff were in desperately short supply and the ward in which I was placed did not have a nurse, but was managed by a few orderlies whose primary task was simply to keep the place clean and tidy and summon the medical staff if they were needed. This may seem a cavalier way in which to run a hospital ward, but most of us under the orderlies' care were quite capable of seeing to our own immediate needs and could be relied upon to help each other out as and when the need arose. The hospital was clean and comfortable and the food was simple and good. A Canadian doctor took charge of my thumb, cleaned and dressed it with a fresh bandage. After a few days no real improvement had taken place, so the bandage was replaced by a plaster cast which stayed on for about a month. However, when the case was finally removed, the top of my thumb had set at a most unusual angle. At this stage I was offered the choice of returning home for proper medical treatment, or letting the doctor have a go at operating on the spot. I opted for the latter: after all, I had come to Spain to fight the Fascists and, so far, I had only spent one day doing so.

When the time came for the operation I walked down to the theatre and lay on a table. A nun was acting as anaesthetist and, having given me a cursory glance, she said:

'Take out tooth.'

'No,' I replied, 'it's not my tooth that needs taking out, it's my thumb that needs fixing.'

'Take out tooth,' she said again, a little more forcefully than before.

'No, it's my thumb,' I said trying hard to match her increasingly authoritarian tone. To add weight to my words I waved the unsightly object rather vigorously in front of her face. Either I had overstepped the mark, or the nun had decided that further conversation was fruitless for without so much as a 'by your leave', she pushed me firmly on to my back, pulled my jaws apart and peered into my mouth. Realization dawned. She had not, after all, been intent on extracting one of my teeth, but was simply anxious that I had no false teeth in place before she gave me the anaesthetic! When, some time later, I came round, my thumb was again encased in plaster. The doctor told me that he had been unable to make good all of the damage which the bullet had inflicted and that I would be left with a shortened, inflexible thumb for the rest of my days. His assessment has since proved correct. Still, he had done his best and I doubt whether any better result would have been achieved had I opted to return to England for surgery.

The nature of my wound did not confine me to the hospital except for a few days and I took advantage of every opportunity to walk through the town and the surrounding countryside in the warm spring sunshine. Murcia was a lovely town with a famous and beautiful cathedral. Of all the religious buildings in the vicinity only the cathedral had not been put to secular use, but had been locked up and placed under guard. All of the other churches had been converted to the production of war material, and were occupied by workers hastily manufacturing uniforms and repairing and converting vehicles. The only building which had been ruthlessly destroyed was the former Law Court. At the time I first saw that devastated building it had little significance to me, but before I left Murcia I was to learn that the town had been the base of a right-wing politician called Juan la Cierva who, in the days before the outbreak of the Civil War, had earned for himself the title of King of the Election Fixers. So famous – or perhaps notorious is a more fitting word – had he become that there was even a saying in popular use to describe his exploits and the power which he had been able to wield, '*Mata al Rey y vente a Murcia*', which roughly translated means 'Kill the king and go to Murcia'; meaning that if the price was right Cierva and his stooges could guarantee anyone immunity from prosecution irrespective of the magnitude of the crime that had been committed. The Law Court had become a symbol of the injustices perpetrated by Cierva and his supporters, and the anger of the people had led to the sacking of a once majestic building.

The town centre of Murcia was like an open-air public library: everywhere there were posters. The most popular depicted a set of prison bars against a simple white background with a hand protruding through the bars, beneath which ran the slogan, 'Amnesty, Vote Communist'. This particular poster was a hangover from the 1936 elections and was one of the most politically adroit that was produced, because it drew the Anarchists, most of whom had not voted before that election, into the political arena. The call for amnesty struck a chord in Anarchist hearts especially as so many of their fellow believers were in prison, as were many others who had been incarcerated after the collapse of the Asturian uprising in 1934. In a way, that poster captured the fragile unity of the Left in Spain, pulling together Anarchists and Communists in a way that had never been possible prior till then.

Murcia was a place of hustle and bustle bathed in almost perpetual sunlight. The irrigated farmland which lay around the town was extremely fertile and produced food in abundance. There was a good market most weekdays selling locally produced fruit and vegetables and no sign of

'panic buying'. Occasionally, after a bull-fight, there would be beef for sale and I would watch the butcher divide the carcase. Every one of his customers would leave his stall with only a pathetically thin strip of meat, and I concluded that some form of voluntary meat rationing was in operation. One of the great difficulties in shopping in the market was in paying for goods, because the middle class of Murcia hoarded every coin. On each stall was a large notice stating, '*No hay cambio*' – we have no change – because there were so few coins in circulation. Elsewhere in war-torn Spain food was far less plentiful, and so the old adage came to be fulfilled. 'If you cannot take the food to the people, bring the people to the food.' In consequence, Murcia had a large and constantly changing population, most of which seemed to participate in the May Day demonstrations in which a number of us from the hospital joined.

During the parade, which was always the highlight of such celebrations, I met a fellow countryman who was serving with the Spanish Navy and who was based at Cartagena. He had been sent to Murcia to collect supplies and invited a group of us to go down to Cartagena to meet a few other English comrades also serving there. As it was no great distance some of us boarded a local bus, packed ourselves in with the peasants and bounced and rolled to the coast. The harbour at Cartagena was magnificent, largely landlocked and with a small entrance to the sea. My spirits fell, however, when I saw the ships. Although I knew next to nothing about warships I knew enough to recognize that the ones belonging to the Republic were very ancient and, I suspected, rather unseaworthy. The pride of the fleet, if that is an accurate description for a ship which looked to have been long past its best, was the *Jaime la Primera*, which had put to sea only to be torpedoed by an Italian submarine lying in wait at the harbour mouth. The crew had managed to bring their ship back to the safety of the harbour but she now stood in dry dock undergoing a lengthy and massive repair operation. Even though we received a warm welcome from the sailors of the fleet and had a great time talking and drinking in the bars with our English comrades I was far from impressed with the fighting capacity of the Navy, not because the men were not keen and capable but simply because of the outdated and outmoded equipment which they were expected to use.

During my last week in Murcia, before I was discharged from the hospital, I went to the local Plaza de Toros to see a bull-fight. Now whilst it is impossible to deny that the pageantry of the bull-fight is impressive, it is equally difficult to deny that the actual fight is hardly congenial to English stomachs. One of the matadors was a very young chap who was

wildly applauded by the crowd when he entered the arena, but from then onward he was on a downward slope. Try as he might, and he certainly tried, he was totally unable to despatch his bull. He repeatedly plunged his sword into the beast's neck but to no effect, and then to add to his confusion and frustration and the crowd's annoyance he lost his grip on his sword. The rapture of his reception had long since been replaced by hearty jeers and catcalls and several young men leapt into the ring, no doubt intent on offering the matador advice, perhaps retrieving the sword, killing the bull, and making a name for themselves all at the same time. The heat of the sun must have taken its toll of me for, before I really knew what I was doing, I was over the fence and into the ring, trying to grab the sweat- and blood-covered tail of the enraged bull, which was charging at anything and everything which moved. Not surprisingly, the ring officials stepped in at this point and cleared all of the amateurs out of the arena before we did some permanent damage to ourselves. Eventually, to a polite and brief round of applause, the rather shamefaced matador did kill the bull, but with little of the finesse which earlier fighters had shown.

Life in Murcia had its lighter side, but what was happening at the front was never far from our thoughts and constantly recurred in our daily conversations. News of the fighting travelled slowly and was not readily come by: local newspapers did carry accounts but we gained only patchy information from them because of our lack of Spanish. In any case wartime newspaper accounts invariably minimize the significance of military setbacks, while tending to overplay the importance of successes, so that an accurate picture is difficult to gauge. While I was at La Pasionaria Hospital the big event of the war was the fighting at Guadalajara. A meeting was called in the hospital courtyard – the only space big enough to hold all of those who attended – to announce the Republican success over the Italian forces. Undoubtedly the Republic did have a major success at Guadalajara: its troops held back the attack of well-trained and vastly experienced professional soldiers who were far superior in mechanized equipment, but it was not the rout that the first reports suggested, for the Italians were not pushed back to their starting-point. Nevertheless, following Jarama, Guadalajara was a significant result for the Republic and guaranteed the security of Madrid for a while longer.

As it was explained to us at the time, the weather had a considerable bearing on the outcome at Guadalajara. The Italians launched their offensive in a spell of prolonged, heavy rain and high winds, which meant that their air support, flying from hastily constructed grass runways, which

quickly turned into quagmires, was soon out of action. The Republican air force, on the other hand, were using a nearby, purpose-built military airfield at Barajas. I do not know how true it was, but we were also told that Mussolini had been so incensed by the failure of his forces that he had issued an order forbidding the repatriation of any of his troops until Italian honour had been vindicated. Certainly I was to encounter more than enough Italian troops in the months ahead!

Upon my discharge from hospital in Murcia in late May, 1937, I returned to Albacete, and from there I immediately proceeded to Morata de Tajuna where the XVth Brigade had established its headquarters. The British Battalion was still occupying very much the same position as it had when I left it three months previously. I assumed my former role of *Enlace* but not with No 3 Company this time. Instead I was attached to Battalion Headquarters and carried messages from the Commanding Officer to the companies at the front. Obviously during my enforced absence certain changes had taken place. Most immediately noticeable were the new faces in the ranks of the Battalion. Of the 600 who had gone into action on the first day of Jarama I doubt if there were more than 100 remaining, and some of these, like myself, had rejoined the Battalion after a period in hospital recovering from wounds. It was astonishing how few of those who had been wounded did manage to rejoin the Battalion. New faces abounded, but people were not getting out from Britain in the same numbers as before. The closing of the frontier between France and Spain by the French Government meant that the route down through Perpignan and into Spain could no longer be used. Instead, the border had to be crossed on foot over the Pyrénées. This was a hazardous undertaking and new recruits who had entered Spain by that tortuous path told hair-raising stories of walking through the high, snow-filled mountain passes in the middle of the night, of falling into gullies and ravines, of damaging ankles, legs and arms, and of being shot at by border patrols. Just to think, I had come by bus!

The shortage of manpower resulting from this despicable action by the French Government meant that the Battalion's four companies were no longer exclusively composed of British nationals. One company was entirely composed of Spaniards. Regrettably, this company was kept separate from the other three. Although there would have been language problems, I always felt that as the Spaniards who enlisted with us and ourselves were fighting a common enemy we should have been completely integrated from the outset.

The advantages of having our Spanish comrades with us soon became

evident. Almost every day they received a variety of newspapers and we could always find someone who could read them and then tell us the latest news. What really endeared the Spanish lads to us, however, was that they had brought along their own cook. This paragon was extremely stout, far too big to be put in a trench, but as he had served as a cook in the Spanish Army before the Civil War he knew how to produce meals under all conditions. I cannot say that he often managed to serve dishes that would rival those of even a modest guest house, but at least every item of food placed before us had been cooked all the way through and occasioned few digestive problems. So highly praised and valued were his somewhat modest offerings that 'cookie' was swiftly elevated to the rank of sergeant and he remained in charge of the Battalion cookhouse until the end of his service with the International Brigades. He was a great character and worth his weight in gold – all seventeen stone of him!

Not only were there new faces in the ranks, but we also had a new Commanding Officer: Fred Copeman. Fred had just about the longest spell of being in command of the Battalion. Ex-British Navy, and a veteran of the Invergordon Mutiny of 1931, he was a real disciplinarian and his firm, almost authoritarian, style was probably one which the Battalion needed most at that time, to ensure that it performed at maximum efficiency and remained an effective fighting force after the severe mauling which it had taken.

We also had a new Brigade Commander, Vladimir Ćopić. As a student, he had been imprisoned for his nationalistic activities. A Croat, Ćopić had served in the Austro-Hungarian Army as an officer during the First World War and had been captured by the Tsarist Army of Nicholas II. From that point onward his political career had been launched, for the Tsarist prisoner-of-war camps were literally universities for Communism. With the success of the Bolshevik Revolution, Ćopić had enlisted in the Red Army and fought in the Russian Civil War. Upon his return to the newly created state of Yugoslavia he was again imprisoned and was finally exiled. He returned to the Soviet Union where he was thoroughly trained in military tactics. As an intelligent man with a great appreciation of the tactics and strategy of warfare, Ćopić was ideally suited to take command of the Brigade. His expertise, coupled with his popularity, assured him of our respect and admiration. Indeed, I cannot recall Ćopić being the subject of criticism. Nevertheless, it was perhaps strange that it was not an Englishman who took command of the XVth, English-speaking, Brigade.

We had some wonderful people serving in Spain, some of whom did not lack military qualifications. One obvious rival for Ćopić's position must have been Major George Nathan, who later served as Chief of Operations at Brunete where he was killed by a Fascist bomb. George looked every inch the military man from his neatly clipped moustache to the swagger stick which he never seemed to put aside. No matter what the conditions, extreme heat or pouring rain, somehow he always managed to look as though he had just walked out of the officer's mess at Sandhurst and on to the parade ground to inspect the troops. George had spent all his life as a soldier and had been a Company Sergeant Major in the British Army during the First World War. Rumour had it that he had later served in Ireland with the Black and Tans, but I have no idea how accurate this was. I have never met anybody who had anything detrimental to say about George and the only regret that most of us had was that he was just one man: we could have used a couple of companies of men of his calibre. Another principal rival for Ćopić's role would have been the American, Major Bob Merriman, of the Lincoln Battalion. Apart from these two there were others who would have been worthy of consideration had the appointment rested solely on courage and not on military training. Fred Copeman, Sam Wild, Bill Alexander, Hugh Slater and Malcolm Dunbar were all men who showed courage which was beyond question and who possessed high qualities of leadership, but they lacked experience of directing large bodies of men under battlefield conditions. So it is difficult to see how Ćopić could have been replaced by a native English-speaking brigade commander, even if it had been thought advisable to do so.

Apart from the changes in personnel, I noted the change in the nature of the battle at Jarama. The all-out offensive and defensive warfare of the early days had been replaced by a far more static form of confrontation. Trenches had been dug and were protected by barbed wire, but the soil in this area was not ideal for trench-digging: it crumbled to dust, so that neat, military-style trenches were not to be seen. Attempts had also been made to build dug-outs as shelter from the sun and rain but, like the trenches, these collapsed at the first artillery bombardment. Nor could the sides of the trenches and dug-outs be shored up with timber, because there was barely enough to feed the cooking stoves. Perhaps wood could have been brought in from other parts of the country, but the army of the Republic was already so hard pressed that little time could be spared for such trivia. The pattern of warfare at Jarama was now one of 'We hold what we have'. Raids on the enemy's trenches took place from time to time in order to capture prisoners who were then interrogated about troop

dispositions and battle plans. There was also sporadic artillery bombardment of our lines, and aircraft would fly from bases situated behind the Fascists' front looking to see if we were moving troops and tanks into position for an offensive. Rarely did we ever see an enemy soldier, although occasionally they would shout insults at us across no-man's-land, especially at night, to which we would reply in kind. Sometimes our political department would bring a van equipped with a loud speaker almost up to the line of the trenches and broadcast Republican songs and slogans. This was a most unpopular exercise with those of us within range of our opponents' guns, because it invariably resulted in our trenches being pounded by their shells, and then the hot, prolonged and tedious task of trench-building had to begin all over again. As we were never sure if the broadcast had been heard by those on the other side of no-man's-land, and as we little expected any change of heart (far more likely that they would pack up and go home if they were within earshot), the loudspeaker van became the object of considerable verbal abuse.

The British Battalion stayed in the line at Jarama until 17th June 1937. We were then relieved and taken by lorry to another of the filthy, little villages which seemed to abound in Spain: Mondejar. The village was not far from Guadalajara so although we were out of the front line it was fairly apparent that we were being held in reserve should another Fascist offensive develop. Mondejar was an Anarchist-controlled village and, as a consequence, its church had been totally destroyed. No thought had been given to putting it to secular use as had happened to the religious buildings in Murcia: the Anarchists had simply vented their anger on all property belonging to the established church with no thought for its possible future use. Despite the fact that Mondejar was hardly a scenic delight, it served as a place in which the Battalion could rest after eighty-seven days in the front line at Jarama. It also allowed us to train the new recruits who had managed to join us after the difficult journey to Spain.

By the end of June we were refreshed and reorganized, and on 2nd July we travelled by lorry to the beautiful foot-hills of the Sierra Guadarrama near San Lorenzo del Escorial, where Philip II had built a huge and magnificent palace. Here we completed our preparations for a forthcoming offensive to the north-west of Madrid. This offensive was an alternative to one initially favoured by certain Ministers within the Republican Government, and which had now fortunately been rejected. It would have involved a large-scale Republican attack in the south, and I understand that certain material, such as bridge-building equipment, had

been stock-piled at Ciudad Real in preparation for that attack. The attack in the south had been envisaged as a sweep across Andalusia to Badajoz, a town 250 miles away on the Portuguese frontier, which had been the scene of a terrific slaughter of Republican forces and civilians in the early days of the insurrection. To get to Badajoz in the middle of summer, across some of the driest parts of Spain, would have presented problems with which the Republic's meagre resources could not have coped. For instance, the advance would have had to have been made on foot because after the first few days air-support could not have been provided, owing to the shortage of aircraft and pilots, and to have moved troops by lorry across open country in daylight would have simply been an open invitation to the Fascists to bomb us and machine-gun us from the air where they

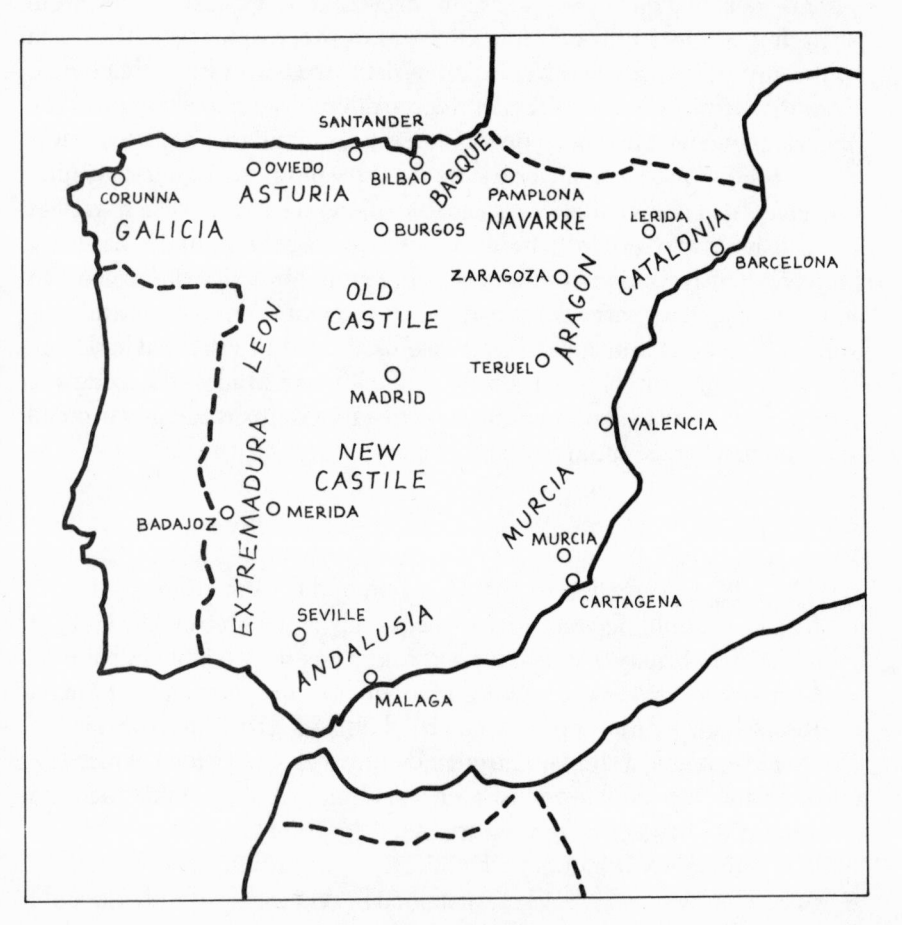

Spain and its regions

would have had an almost unchallenged supremacy. In addition, there was the consideration that to protect a spearhead seeking an objective 250 miles away would have involved numerous secondary offensives on its flanks to prevent it being cut-off, encircled and destroyed. I am sure that the Republic simply didn't possess the manpower necessary for such an operation, and that this was the reason why it was abandoned in favour of the attack to the north-west of Madrid for which we were preparing.

At San Lorenzo del Escorial we had a few glorious days of sunbathing and soaking in the little, cool streams which flowed down into the valleys from the high, snow-capped Sierra Guadarrama which towered above the village. On 5th July, our rest and relaxation came to an end and we began to move up on foot to take our position for the forthcoming attack. At Jarama our objective had been to prevent the Fascist forces from encircling Madrid. Our new objective was to sweep down from the north of the city and move up behind the Fascist forces, who were attacking it from the west – and thus prevent their artillery from continuing to shell Madrid, now virtually under siege. Perhaps of secondary importance, was the realization that such an attack would show, both to our enemy and to ourselves, that the Republic was capable of waging an offensive as well as a defensive war. Certainly the prospect of taking the initiative after the bloody defensive action at Jarama and the period of stalemate which had followed the first three hectic days of ferocious fighting there, was sufficient to boost our morale and give us a sense of eager anticipation. We were going into battle again, but this time we would be making the running, rather than simply responding to a Fascist thrust. Now we would show them what we could do.

* * *

The role played by the British Battalion of the XVth International Brigade in holding what was subsequently labelled 'Suicide Hill' on 12th February 1937 had been a key factor in containing the Nationalist thrust across the Jarama. To the north elements of the Republican Army supported by the XIth and XIIth International Brigades staged a similar rearguard action west of Arganda, which, by 16th February, had forced General Orgaz to concede that there was little prospect of cutting the Madrid-Valencia highway. For the Nationalists it had been an expensive campaign for very little gain. The Army of Africa had sustained heavy casualties with 6,000 men killed and was never again used as a spearhead assault unit.

Furthermore, while the German artillery had shown itself to devastating effect, the Soviet T–26 tanks and Polikarpov 1–15 aircraft had consistently outfought their German and Italian adversaries. The battle was therefore acclaimed as a victory for the Republic, for after an initial setback it had quickly marshalled its forces to contain the Nationalist thrust. What such an assessment ignored, however, was that the Nationalist advance was only held by the Republic transferring seventy-four Battalions plus a Soviet tank brigade to confront a Nationalist force of forty battalions plus fifteen cavalry squadrons. Furthermore, the Republican Army which was cast in the defensive role sustained losses of approximately 10,000 men. Clearly it was a victory bought at a cost, and despite the heroism of the Republican infantry the course of the battle had largely been determined by the ability, on this occasion, of the Soviet supplied tanks and aircraft to overawe their opponents. With the build-up of German and Italian equipment in the following months the Republic had enjoyed a military superiority, particularly in the air, which was rarely to be repeated in future engagements.

The Battle of Jarama did not, however, mark the end of Franco's attempts to capture Madrid. On 8th March 1937 a further assault was launched to the north-east of the capital with the intention of cutting the Madrid-Zaragoza highway and eventually driving south to link with a renewed offensive across the Jarama in a pincer movement which would encircle the city. The spearhead force had been supplied by 30,000 Italian troops, who had recently played a major role in the capture of Malaga, supported by 15,000 Nationalist soldiers. Organized into four motorized divisions the Italians intended to break through on a forty-mile-wide front and, supported by Italian and German aircraft, quickly drive south to capture Guadalajara. After initial success in penetrating the Republican lines up to a depth of thirty miles the Italian advance was halted on 13th March by reinforcements hastily rushed from the Jarama. With poor weather denying the Italians air support and bogging down their motorized columns, the initiative quickly passed to the battle-hardened Republican brigades moving up from the south supported by Soviet tanks and aircraft. Over the course of the next week the Italians were pushed back almost to their starting-point with a loss of 2,000 men. Only the slowness of the Republic to exploit its success prevented a complete rout. As it

was the Italians were hastily withdrawn from the line and replaced by Nationalist troops no doubt much to the contempt of their Spanish allies.

The battle of Guadalajara finally persuaded Franco that the build-up of Republican forces in Madrid was on such a scale that further assaults on the capital were pointless. The Nationalists, therefore, turned their attention to the Republican enclave on the northern coast of Spain consisting of Santander, Asturias and the Basque province of Vizcaya. This region was of both political and economic importance, in that areas of it were heavily industrial-ized, holding vast iron ore and coal reserves as well as containing the key port of Bilbao. In addition the Asturians were amongst the most ardent supporters of the Republic and Franco appreciated that their defeat would represent a stunning psychological blow to the Republican cause. On 30th March 1937 General Mola threw over 40,000 troops with extensive air and artillery support against the Basques. The defenders fought tenaciously but were handi-capped from the outset by internal rivalry between the various provinces which prevented the creation of a unified command. Furthermore, cut off from the main Republican forces concen-trated around Madrid, they were deprived of the Soviet tank and air support which had been so important in determining events of Jarama and Guadalajara. In particular the Basques had no answer to the firepower of the German Condor Legion which graphically demonstrated its destructive prowess by demolishing the town of Guernica on 26th April 1937. Over a period of two months the Basque defensive positions crumbled in the face of the Nationalist onslaught. On 19th June 1937 Bilbao fell to the advancing forces of General Davila, General Mola having been killed in an aeroplane accident on 3rd June 1937.

The allegiance of the Basques to the Republic had, from the outset, been tenuous in that they were devout Catholics and therefore would have little truck with the anti-clerical excesses which were a marked feature of the Republican movement in Catalonia and Madrid. Their support for the Republic was thus largely based upon its willingness to recognize the right of the province to a form of autonomy and semi-independence from Madrid. The Asturians, however, had always been amongst the most fervent advocates of radical social and political reform and from the beginning of the war had sought to destroy the power and

position of the Church and collectivize all forms of private property. Therefore, as the Nationalists advanced west into Santander and the Asturias there was mounting pressure on the Republic to open a counter-offensive to relieve the pressure on the northern front.

It appeared that several options were open to the Republican Army. The most adventurous scheme was a major thrust south-west of Madrid into the province of Extremadura to seize the town of Merida. Such an attack would have sidestepped the major Nationalist troop concentrations, and by driving to the Portuguese border would have cut the territory held by Franco into two separate enclaves. Furthermore, it would have denied the northern Nationalist armies of supplies from their Mediterranean ports and would have cut Franco's key supply route from Portugal. An alternative was provided by an operation in north-east Spain on the Aragon front. An assault designed to push the Nationalist forces out of Aragon promised not only to liberate Zaragoza, the spiritual home of Spanish anarchism, but also to apply more immediate pressure to the Nationalist forces moving against Santander. The third option was once again to reopen hostilities around Madrid in the hope of gaining either a substantial victory against the bulk of the Nationalist army, which was still encamped to the west of the capital, or at least forcing Franco to withdraw troops from the northern campaign.

It was this last option which was finally adopted.

3

The Battles of Brunete and Belchite

An offensive in the vicinity of Madrid had the advantage of being staged at a point where the Republican Army was already massed in strength, and, following its successes at Jarama and Guadalajara, local commanders were confident of their ability to take the offensive against the Nationalists. More cynical observers, however, were later to comment that the decision was probably influenced by the determination of the military commanders in the Madrid region and their Soviet advisers to retain complete control over all major offensives mounted by the Republic, and therefore they automatically opposed campaigns in either northern or southern Spain. In the first week of July the cream of the Republican army was massed north of Madrid with the intention of driving south through the Nationalist lines to the west of Madrid, initially to capture the village of Brunete, and eventually to cut Franco's key supply route to Merida. If the opening assault was successful a further force would strike north from the southern suburbs of the capital to complete a pincer movement which would encircle the Nationalist forces besieging Madrid.

The attack opened at dawn on 6th July 1937 with a force of tanks and infantry penetrating the Nationalist lines on a ten-mile front. It was anticipated that Brunete would be captured by ten a.m., for up to 50,000 Republican troops were only opposed by 2,000 Nationalists concentrated in small strongholds at villages between Brunete and the front line. The XVth International Brigade, containing the British Battalion, was to be kept in reserve during the initial assault, but following the fall of Villanueva de la Canada it would push forward with the XIIIth International Brigade to cut the road connecting Brunete with Madrid. When, however, by early afternoon Villanueva de la Canada had still not fallen to the Republican tanks and infantry, it was apparent that the pace of the

66

advance had been seriously misjudged. With the element of surprise rapidly ebbing away, and with the cream of the Republican Army committed to an assault on a dangerously narrow front, the XVth International Brigade was thrown into the assault on the fortified village of Villanueva de la Canada.

* * *

On that morning of 6th July, we in the British Battalion began moving over the hilly countryside towards the fortified village of Villanueva de la Canada. The mid-summer heat was almost unbearable and the dust which our boots threw into the air with every stride caught at our throats and produced a raging thirst. Flies swarmed around us in clouds, adding to our misery. The Republic was committing 50,000 men to an offensive on a fairly small front. 50,000 men fouling the atmosphere wherever they went, with no time to dig proper latrines and no water to spare for washing the sweat and grime from their bodies and clothes. No wonder we were plagued by flies: they must have thought that all their birthdays had come at once! To overcome the problems of thirst we were told to find a small, smooth pebble and suck it. After trying this remedy I quickly abandoned it as it did nothing to quench my desire to drink a bucketful of water, and I seemed to be in constant danger of swallowing the blessed thing every time I took a deep breath. As though out of nowhere we suddenly came across a refugee family. If there is anything I hate on a battlefield it is children and horses, and here I had both of them at once. The family had obviously packed up everything they possessed and thrown it into their horse-drawn cart at the first sign of trouble, and were now intent on making good their escape to safety; and who could blame them? Shells from the enemy guns were falling all around us, causing the horses pulling the cart to panic, and a man was holding the reins of the leading horse while his wife hung on like grim death to the neck of its companion. They had blindfolded the horses so that they would not rush off in headlong flight at the sight of the exploding shells, and the husband was frantically trying to find out from some of our Spanish comrades which way he should go to escape the bombardment. They were busy telling him to get off the road to avoid our tanks, and that his family would be safer away from us as we were likely to attract considerable attention from the Fascist air force. I looked at the cart all piled up with the family's meagre possessions, and seated at the back of it, surrounded by her own personal belongings, was dear old grandma. A real Spanish grandma, dressed from

head to foot in black with a thick woollen shawl pulled tightly around her. She could have come straight off a canvas in the Prado. She was running a rosary between her fingers at a prodigious rate and looking far from content with her lot. Peering from one side of the cart with big, brown, frightened eyes was a girl about eight years old and from the other side there protruded the head of her six-year-old brother, bursting with excitement and by far the least troubled member of the family. Fascination at meeting so many soldiers must have replaced any fear which he may have felt from the shelling. The boy stretched out his hand to touch my rifle but grandma snatched him back. I bet he thought I was a real soldier! I talked to the kiddies in my very limited and halting Spanish and rummaged around in my pockets to see if I could find them a few sweets. The ones which I did eventually manage to offer them were very sticky and speckled with dust, but the children were more than happy to pop them into their mouths. I often think of that family and especially of the kids. I think that somewhere in Spain there is a woman – she is probably a grandma herself by now – who will be telling her grandchildren about how, as a young girl, she was on a battlefield and a soldier from overseas, with blue eyes and cheeks tanned deep brown by a sun the like of

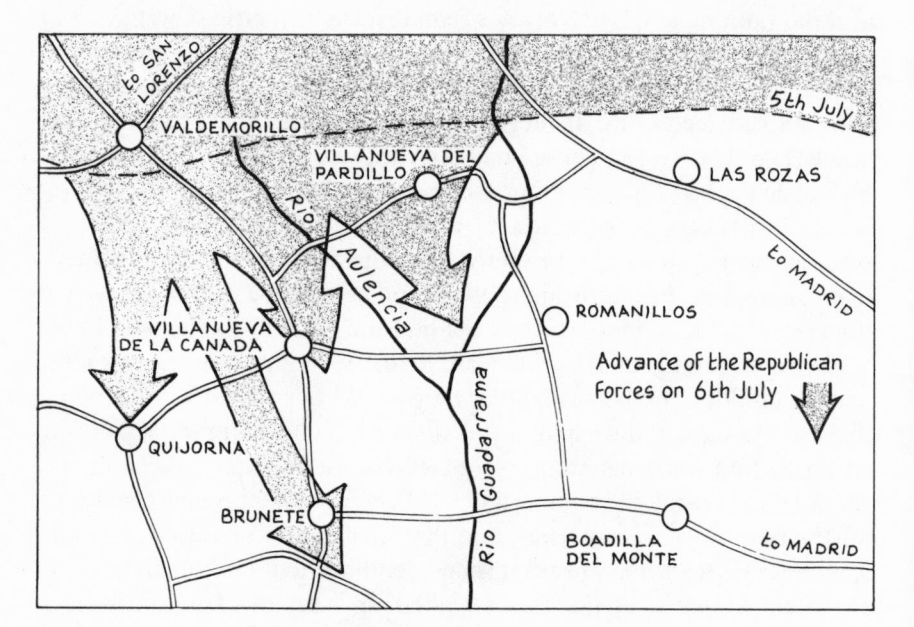

Map B: Republican Assault on the First Day
of the Battle of Brunete 6th July 1937

which he had never seen, had given her a rather grubby and sticky sweet. I can picture the incredulity of her audience: ' . . . as if Grandma was ever on a battlefield, what a joke . . . !' I said '*Hasta la vista*' to the children, but I bet that they never thought that I would escape death.

Having made sure that the refugee family was well clear of the road, we swung round toward our objective, Villanueva de la Canada. Although we did not know it at the time, Brunete had fallen to our troops somewhat earlier, but there was still a considerable pocket of Fascist resistance at Villanueva de la Canada. First we had to isolate the village by cutting off the road on its southern side – to prevent a relief column making an unwelcome arrival on the scene and to restrict the possibility of enemy troops escaping from their fortified positions when we made things a little too hot for them. With the road cut we began a cautious advance toward the village itself which, like nearly all Spanish villages, had a church towering above the other buildings. As we drew closer we were subjected to a murderous hail of machine-gun fire from well-sited guns on top of the church. I threw myself into a roadside ditch and began to crawl forward on all fours toward the village.

Throughout the march from the environs of San Lorenzo del Escorial, I had been in the compnay of a Welsh comrade. He had rabbited on interminably about how when the war was over I had to go and visit him and how he would take me to a pub which he knew in a green Welsh valley. He eulogized over this pub and described it so vividly that, in the dreadful heat and dust and plagued almost beyond endurance by the flies, I too came to see his favourite hostelry. I could clearly visualize the dark-haired barmaid plonking the pints of beer on to the counter and the foam easing its way over the top of the glass, creeping slowly down the sides, and soaking into the towelling which lay along the top of the bar. Taffy had nearly driven me frantic with thoughts of such delights. When I had dived for the safety of the roadside ditch he had been right behind me and now, safe from the fire of the machine-guns, I turned to look for him.

'Are you all right, Taff?'

There was no reply.

I worked my way back along the ditch and saw him lying on his face. I rolled him on to his side. He was dead. A bullet had gone through his forehead. His mouth hung open and was full of flies. His tongue, which had swollen from thirst, was protruding. His eyes were still open and covered with those blasted flies which were also working their way into his ears. It is a picture which has stayed with me for forty-five years and one which I am certain will never leave my consciousness. If the heat and

excitement of battle had overcome the fear and tension that I felt before going into action, there was also little time for compassion or remorse and I can only remember thinking, 'Good Heavens, he's dead, and I don't know where the pub is.'

It was only when I reached for my rifle and started to crawl back along the ditch again that I noticed that blood was dripping out of my shirt-sleeve. I rolled on to my back and pulled up my sleeve and saw that a bullet had passed cleanly and neatly through the fleshy part of my arm just above the elbow, which was already starting to stiffen and turn all the colours of the rainbow. Had the same bullet which had passed unnoticed through my arm continued on its way to kill Taff? Funny things happen in war but I think that was more than a little unlikely. Still, who knows? I decided to take a breather and dress my wound before attempting to catch up with the rest of the company which had by now moved on some way ahead. It was while I was busy fixing a temporary dressing that I heard voices behind me. I looked back to an olive grove which we had passed through earlier and saw there a cavalry patrol which was calling me to join it. I could not make out whether the mounted men were wearing our uniforms or those of the Fascist forces, so I decided to ignore them. I am not sure if the cavalrymen knew which side I belonged to but they fired a few rounds at me, all of which missed, before riding off.

Having fixed the dressing to my arm I crawled forward to rejoin the Battalion which was spread out along a ditch within rifle range of the village. It was the very devil fighting in that heat with no protection from the sun's searing rays. Accurate shooting was impossible because everything was shimmering. The Fascist machine-gunners had no such problem, as all they had to do was to spray bullets around with gay abandon; but rifle-men were shooting at targets which never held still for a second. All day we stayed in that ditch, ducking down low whenever a machine-gun swung in our direction and sprayed us with bullets, popping up as soon as it had traversed away and firing back with every weapon at our disposal. It was an awfully long day and as it wore on I found it progressively more difficult to steady my rifle as my arm became increasingly inflexible.

At dusk there was a commotion in the village and all of those around me started to peer over the top of the ditch to see what was happening. A party of women and children were slowly leaving the village and making their way down the road toward our position. They were closely packed together and casting fearful and anxious glances to left and right as they moved forward. We started yelling at them to get a move on, to get away

from the village as fast as possible, to get off the road where they were so visible, to get behind our lines where they would have some protection. As they drew nearer we saw that they were being used as a human shield by a group of Fascist troops who were crouching behind them and forcing them forward, in tight formation, at bayonet-point. These heroes then started firing at us from behind their living armour and we had no alternative but to return their fire. With great regret I have to state that quite a few of those poor women and their children were killed and wounded by both Fascist and Republican bullets which missed their intended targets. It was a side of war that I had never seen before and, thank God, I was never to see again. How the self-proclaimed saviours of Spain could have sunk to such depths of inhumanity defies any explanation that I am able to offer.

By nightfall my arm had stiffened so much that try as I might, and I certainly tried, I could no longer fire my rifle with any hope of hitting anyone or anything except by a stroke of great good fortune; and what I had seen of the fighting that day did not suggest to me that good fortune was in plentiful supply. As at Jarama, it was time for me to take myself out of the front line and seek proper medical treatment. I reported my injury to Fred Copeman and left the fray. In the dark I cautiously worked my way around the village and back to the main road where I was able to climb aboard an ambulance taking the less seriously wounded to Madrid. Before dawn I was in a hospital on the Calle de Velasquez near a famous spot in Madrid called the Puerta de Alcala, one of the old gates of the city and just off the Calle Alcala. Calvo Sotelo, a notable monarchist politican before the Insurrection, had lived in a house on the Calle de Velasquez. Sotelo's assassination by Republican supporters in July 1936 in reprisal for the murder of Teniente Jose Castillo of the Asaltos, had played a key part in triggering off the Civil War. The Calle de Velasquez was in an extremely fashionable, residential part of the city and was an ideal place in which to situate a hospital, since the Fascist gunners, who were submitting the capital to an almost ceaseless artillery barrage, aimed principally at the working-class areas and targets of a military nature. The whole area between the Castellana and the Retiro Park was a 'safe' zone and, as all the former inhabitants had fled, their beautiful homes were being used as refugee hostels or, in certain cases, as hospitals. However, the Republican artillery was based in the Retiro Park and frequently fired over our heads at the Fascist positions west of Madrid and at enemy artillery around Mount Garabitas. Inevitably our heavy guns attracted return fire but fortunately most of the incoming shells passed overhead,

leaving our little enclave relatively safe. At least the local children thought so as they played in the streets with total unconcern. In consequence, we were only troubled by an infrequent, poorly aimed shell. The hospital itself was beautifully clean and remarkably comfortable and there was little wrong with my arm that a few days' rest would not put to rights. Again, I had been lucky in avoiding any infection in the wound, but I did feel that I was proving to be far too attractive a target for the Fascist sharpshooters.

An English nursing-sister was in charge of the hospital. This was not due to a shortage of doctors, but had arisen because only walking wounded with minor injuries, requiring the minimum of surgical treatment, were assigned there. It was the sister who let slip a strong rumour that a bar in the Puerta del Sol had received a consignment of beer. In a besieged city like Madrid such a rumour was treated most seriously and a small group of us from the hospital decided that it warranted empirical verification. The Puerta del Sol lay at the far end of the Calle Alcala, parts of which were being subjected to fairly regular artillery fire. Undeterred, we set off in search of the precious commodity, sprinting from doorway to doorway, or throwing ourselves flat on the ground whenever we heard the roar of an approaching shell. It was a bit like a bizarre game of musical chairs with the devil playing the tune; all quiet, run like hell looking for a doorway; shell coming, dive into the doorway and make yourself as small and inconspicuous as possible; all quiet, so off again. At times glass and roofing tiles, torn loose by an exploding shell, flew wildly across the street and people who had been injured cried out for help. Finally, we made it to the Puerta del Sol, which was the social centre of the city, and much to our joy we found that the rumour was true.

The beer was deliciously cool, but we were restricted to two glasses each. But delightful though it was, it was hardly worth the risks we had run to reach it and, besides, we still had to make the same hazardous journey back to the hospital. I resolved never to be so foolhardy again. If I was going to die in Spain, then it would be on a battlefield. What if I was killed in Madrid and details of my demise reached my family? I could just imagine the scene that would take place at home in Nottingham.

'I'm sorry, but I have to tell you that Walter has been killed in Madrid.'

'In which particular action did he die?'

'Well actually, he was going for a glass of beer in a small bar near the city centre at the time. . . . '

No, I think the people back home wanted and expected something

better than that from me. Such sombre thoughts were, however, unnecessary as all of the drinkers managed safely to negotiate the return journey to the comfort of their hospital wards.

Quite close to my hospital was the famous group of statues called Las Cibeles, well-known to all visitors to Madrid, but during the war protected from stray shells by a huge wall of sandbags. The need to safeguard the national heritage is fully understandable but given the shortage of hessian bags that existed in Spain and the dire need of them in the front line I always viewed their use in this way with mixed feelings.

A frequent sight in the area of Las Cibeles was that of the Women's Militia coming on and off duty. In twos and threes they would make their way down the Grand Via which ultimately led to the University City and the Madrid front line. The Grand Via was too often shelled to be used by vehicles nor could the women have risked marching down its length in formation. In small groups and chattering away to each other they looked very like women the world over and only their dishevelled khaki uniforms after several nights in the trenches marked them out as being something special. These brave girls were such a common sight that they did not attract comment nor did they appear to want to. Yet Madrid remained the only place in Spain where I saw women in the front line, although it must be remembered that the first British subject killed in the war was Felicia Browne who died on the Aragon Front as early as 25th August 1936.

Within a couple of days I felt that my arm would not handicap me at the front and I asked the sister to discharge me from her care.

With my arm heavily strapped I rejoined the Battalion near Brunete as it fought to repel the Fascist counter-attacks. Although we had support from Soviet-made tanks and, at least for the first few days, the Republican air force was to be seen bombing and strafing the enemy's positions, the Battalion received a terrible battering.

The suffering from heat and thirst was dreadful. Every day I thought of the old brass tap above the sink at home with the cool, clear water gushing from it. Even when that tap was turned off water still dripped from it and this now seemed like the most unbelievable waste! I promised myself that should I ever return home one of the first things I would do would be to plunge my head under the water flowing from that tap! Hunger was another constant companion whenever we engaged the enemy, for their artillery and aircraft always obstructed our supply lorries during daylight. Food trucks could only reach us after dark when they had to compete with all of the other vehicles carrying materials to the front. In the ensuing chaos, we often went hungry. Sometimes we would get our food just

before dawn, which inevitably started a discussion as to whether this meal belonged to the previous day or to today, and someone could be guaranteed to remember which meals he had received in the last few days; or to be more precise, which meals he had not received and what he thought the cookhouse owed him. Then, in the dark, when rations were being hastily issued from a lorry's tailboard, you could hear a babble of European languages in the queue for food, since troops who had been separated from their units in the confusion of battle had attached themselves to us; at least at mealtimes. This we did not mind as long as everyone got something to eat.

Day after day was spent in firing, hiding, firing again and hiding again, and all of the time the sun beat remorselessly down, the dust clutched at our throats, the flies drove us wild, and our losses climbed inexorably upwards. When the Battalion paraded at the end of the offensive on 26th July, only forty-two men, including cookhouse staff, answered the roll-call out of the 600 who had gone into the attack just under three weeks before. Some 550 of our comrades were dead, wounded or missing. Of those not on parade, a few who had been wounded later rejoined the Battalion at its base at Mondejar where we were sent after a short stay back at San Lorenzo del Escorial.

By any standards the Battalion had taken a severe mauling at Brunete. I am sure that the ferocious response of the Fascists to our attack, which again resulted in us fighting a defensive battle, was largely due to the fact that Franco was incensed by our audacity in moving on to the offensive and that he was determined to defeat us and break our morale once and for all.

Towards the end of July 1937 I was so ill and exhausted from the effects of heat, thirst and hunger and lack of sleep that I expected the enemy simply to surge forward and overwhelm us. So many of my comrades shared my physical plight that we had lost the power to resist a determined assault. What I did not appreciate was the fact that our enemy had fared no better, and, that despite the enthusiasm of the Fascist Commander, General Inglesias Varela, for an all-out attack, General Franco would not release the fresh troops needed for such a venture. Dr George Hills portrays the situation so very accurately in *The Battle for Madrid* that it is worth quoting his description,

Apart from the normal hardship of battle, aerial and artillery bombardment by day and night, deafening noise, the sickly smell of decomposing bodies, the acrid smoke of burning stubble, the physical

effort of attack and hand-to-hand fighting. The sun had beaten mercilessly day in day out, and the nights had been airless. Neither side's supply columns had been equipped to carry enough drinking water, and there had been cases on both sides of men going mad with thirst.

It would be impossible to state the position more precisely.

Fortunately for us, Franco also had an obsession with winning the war in the north of the country which outweighed his desire to smash us at Brunete, and so he pulled out much of his artillery which was ranged against us and sent it off to Asturias. That decision enabled us to stabilize the Brunete front. Had Franco done as some of his generals advocated and continued the action at Brunete, I fear that we would have been pushed right back into the streets of Madrid.

Despite this error of judgement, however, Franco had succeeded temporarily in lowering our morale. It was a very small and dispirited group of troops who returned to Mondejar. Our morale had received something of a boost while we rested at San Lorenzo and waited for the lorries which were to take us back to our base. To take our minds off the horror of reliving the sight of our comrades being killed and wounded, we organized a football match. While we were playing two big private cars drew up and an officer, complete with an armed bodyguard, stepped from the leading car and walked toward us. We had no time to smarten ourselves up or collect our equipment before we were face-to-face with General Miaja, Commander of the Republican forces on the Madrid Front. He asked us to which battalion we belonged, and when we told him he quietly moved forward and shook all of us by the hand and praised us for our bravery murmuring, '*Muy valiente, muy valiente*'. I have been told that Miaja was nicknamed 'Papa' by those who served under him in the Spanish Army and I can believe that, for he appeared a most kind and gentle sort of man. He wore no gold braid or medals and he left his hat and his bodyguard in the car. He just came over to us unobtrusively and, although we did not possess enough Spanish to have a conversation with him, we were left with the impression that he really cared about us, that we were something more to him than simply a flag on a map which he could move about as he chose. Miaja had been one of the highest-ranking officers to remain loyal to the Republic and he must have had more than his share of personal courage, because he had gone out on the streets of Madrid in November and December 1936, months when the militia was in chaos and retreating from the Fascist advance, rallied it, organized it,

and put it back in the front line. A brave man and a humane man, and I was very pleased that I had that one brief meeting with him. It meant a lot to me at the time and it still does to this day.

On our return to Mondejar a number of meetings, organized by the Battalion's Political Commissar, were held, at which we tried to assess the events and effects of our offensive at Brunete. At these meetings everyone was free to speak without any fear of recrimination. Of course we blamed Hitler, we blamed Mussolini, we blamed the Non Intervention Committee, and we blamed ourselves for making mistakes. How easy it is to be wise after the event. One thing we had overlooked, and upon which we were all agreed, was how essential it was to store adequate supplies of water in terrain where it was at a premium. At Brunete, our lack of water had led to a great deal of unnecessary suffering, and water had become an obsession. One night, with the Battalion safely settled on a low hill, I had been put in charge of a platoon and sent to guard a nearby dry river bed, a *barranco*. By digging into the dusty shale of the river course you could make a small hole which would gradually fill with a whitish liquid – which did not really merit the description of 'water'. It was foul to drink and if drunk by the mouthful had disastrous effects upon the bowels. Provided that it was only used very sparingly to moisten the lips and tongue, then it did not seem to produce any ill-effects. As this constituted the nearest supply of water to the Battalion I was ordered to make sure that it did not fall into enemy hands. My instructions to the platoon were simple. 'If you hear any sound of movement from the river throw a hand grenade in that direction.' Although the Fascists were better provisioned than us, they fully appreciated the importance of threatening our fragile water supply.

While many of the criticisms voiced at the meetings organized by the Battalion's Political Commissar were far from constructive, the meetings themselves were a help in that they revealed the many unforced errors we had made and strengthened our resolve not to commit them again in the future. Having discovered the causes of our failures and the means by which to correct them, the meetings left us with the feeling that we could make significant improvements on our past performance. Also, the mere act of participating in the post-battle analysis helped to forge a common bond, an *esprit de corps*, and a sense of unity of purpose which might not otherwise have so readily emerged.

Our return to Mondejar was in sharp contrast to the noisy enthusiasm the villagers had shown at our departure. Then, they had seen a strong, optimistic battalion setting out to do battle with the Fascists, and they must have thought that a Republican victory was as good as guaranteed.

Now they witnessed a small band of weary and despondent men gathering back at base. It must have been unnerving for them to see such a transformation in so short a time. But gradually our numbers grew as new recruits joined us, and the less badly wounded returned from hospital. In an attempt to boost our morale and that of the villagers we organized some concerts. What effect these impromptu performances had on the locals I shudder to think, but I am sure that they were of much less importance than the presence of the Battalion doctor. In those days, very few Spanish villages had a resident qualified doctor. The best that the stoical agrarian workers could hope for was that a *practicante*, someone who could dispense a few pills and who had some knowledge of herbal remedies, would decide to make his home with them. It was, therefore, an occasion of great rejoicing when our doctor delivered a local woman of twins. Never in living memory had the birth of two babies at the same time proved so easy, and the simple, kindly people of Mondejar were unable to conceal their delight.

Within two to three weeks the Battalion had been brought back to its fighting strength of around 600 men. All of the new recruits had received some basic training, including rifle practice and were reasonably well equipped with footwear and uniforms and a blanket in which to sleep. Some of the old hands after brief spells in hospital again assumed their places in the ranks and the return of these veterans raised our spirits. Peter Daly had taken over the command of the Battalion because Fred Copeman had been forced to give up, as his wounds had got the better of him. Peter was one of our Irish comrades and I would suspect that his knowledge of military strategy and tactics was no greater than that of our previous commanders, but he had that easy-going nature and lack of reserve which seem to be a feature of many Irishmen and his was a popular appointment.

In the middle of August our Battalion was moved north to the Aragon Front. In the heat of a Spanish mid-summer this long, dusty journey by lorry proved both wearisome and wearing, but we had little time to recharge our batteries in the small village of Azaila before going into action at Quinto. The terrain there was the very worst: bleak, exposed, unproductive, treeless hillsides which offered no protection from the elements and scant cover from enemy fire. It was a dreadful and dreary landscape which seemed to gnaw into one and erode the spirit. Our American comrades of the Lincoln-Washington Battalion moved to take the small township of Quinto. But protecting the town and commanding the main road through the Ebro Valley from Zaragoza was the natural

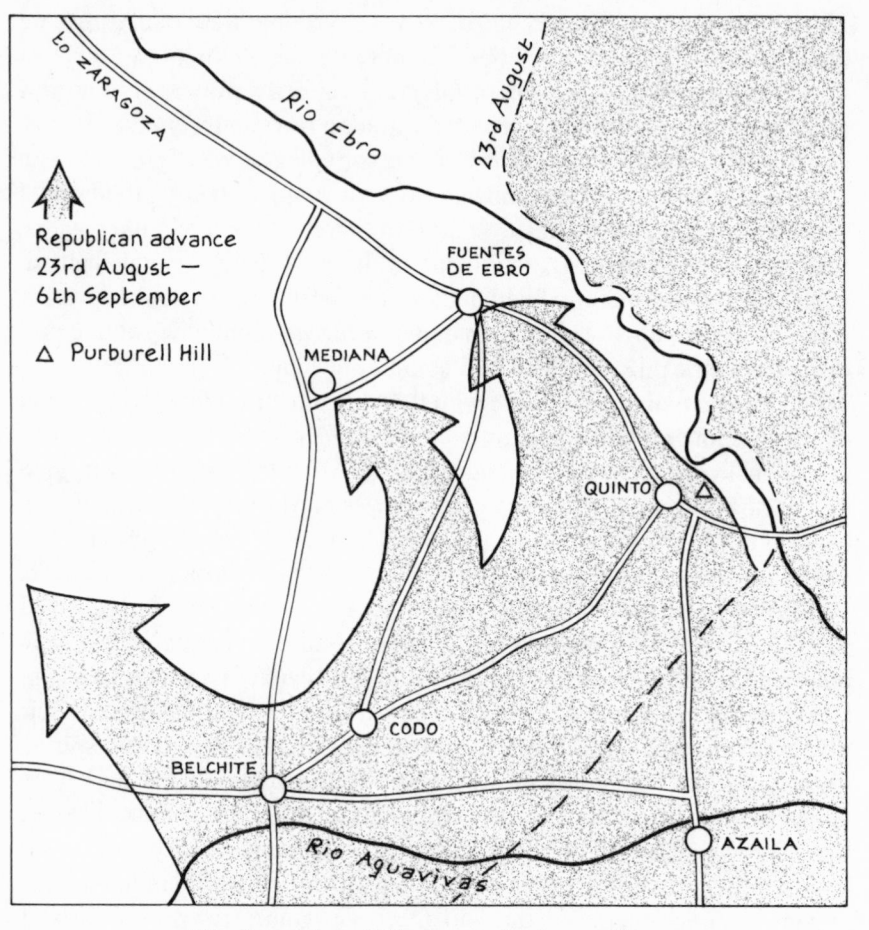

The Republican Offensive on the Aragon Front
August 1937

vantage-point of Purburell Hill and it fell to the British Battalion to take
and secure this strategic landmark. Although we were told that Purburell
Hill was not heavily defended, this information proved to be inaccurate:
indeed, Purburell Hill had been skilfully fortified by German engineers.

The strong fortifications and the ferocious resistance we encountered
were the two most memorable military aspects of the Aragon Campaign
and were related because of a strange paradox. The paradox centred on
Zaragoza, the largest town in the province. In the days before the outbreak
of the Civil War, Zaragoza had been the home of the Anarchist movement
in Aragon. Even the Catalonian Anarchists had held their conferences

there. But within a few days of the Insurrection the town had fallen to the Fascists because its garrison had thrown in its lot with Franco and had successfully resisted the efforts of the local militia to unseat it. The retaking of Zaragoza had become a matter not only of strategy but emotion: the town had become both a military and a symbolic target and Durruti's Anarchist forces had made repeated efforts to fight their way up the Ebro Valley and return Zaragoza to the Republic.* The fighting in Aragon was, therefore, also an ideological confrontation and this, probably more than any other single factor, accounted for the vicious nature of the fighting, since the opposing forces were totally committed to incompatible ideologies. To the Fascist defenders, the retention of their hold on Zaragoza was a symbol of their impending triumph; to the Republican attackers, the town's continuing occupation by their sworn enemy was a running sore in their flesh, that they had pledged themselves to cure. Both sides were only too clearly aware of the vehemence of their opponent's challenge, and, as the Fascists were in possession, they had made good use of this advantage to prepare well-designed fortifications surrounded by barbed wire, a multitude of slit trenches and gun emplacements. Care had also been taken to camouflage many of their positions so that they could not be readily spotted from the air.

Purburell Hill proved to be a case in point. Expecting little resistance, the British Battalion began its ascent of the steep hillside, only to be met by a murderous machine-gun fire. We sought what natural cover there was, every undulation in the rocky ground, no matter how insignificant it appeared at a first, casual glance, housed one or more men trying to bury themselves in the unyielding earth to avoid the bullets which flew ceaselessly overhead. Rifles and hand-grenades were useless against the armaments massed on the higher ground above us. Our Commander Peter Daly was wounded in the opening moments of our initial attack and later died of his injuries in hospital at Beni Casim. Those of us fortunate enough to have survived the first onslaught sought what protection we could, as throughout a long, hot and bloody day we waited for the sun to go down and the arrival of darkness to shield our retreat from those bullet-swept slopes. Many died before nightfall gave us the protection we so desperately needed to fall back and regroup. With Paddy O'Daire now

*Buenaventura Durruti (1876–1936), legendary Anarchist who led a column of 2,000 Anarchist militia in an attempt to recapture Zaragoza from the Fascists in July–August 1936. Killed fighting on the Madrid front on 20th November 1936. The 'Durruti Column' was subsequently absorbed into the Republican Army as the Anarchist 26th Division.

in command, we licked our wounds beyond the range of the defenders' guns.

During the night a Fascist patrol blundered into our hastily prepared positions at the foot of the hill, and we took them prisoner. Our interrogation of them revealed that although our opponents possessed men, food and ammunition in plenty, and were safe in their carefully prepared trenches and dug-outs, they had made the elementary and atrocious mistake of not securing a source of water for themselves. The patrol we had captured was weighed down with empty water containers, and admitted that if we were simply to maintain a cordon around the foot of Purburell Hill, it would fall to us eventually, as even the best trained and most lavishly equipped troops could not hold a position in the heat of a Spanish summer without a plentiful supply of water. But time was at a premium, and the success of the Aragon Campaign depended on our being able to bring men and supplies to the front along the Ebro Valley, and the valley was dominated by the guns on Purburell Hill.

So, before dawn next morning, we were moving upward once again, but this time we were far better prepared than we had been on the previous day. Not only did we bring our machine-guns up to support our advance, but we also had the Brigade's Anti-Tank Battery which played a decisive role. The anti-tank gun was a most useful weapon. Although it had only a small calibre it also had a low trajectory and it was used most effectively to pound the Fascist machine-gun emplacements and barbed-wire higher up the slopes for two or three hours before the infantry went into attack. The anti-tank crew did their work well and when we surged to the crest of the hill we met nothing approaching the lethal barrage of fire that we had encountered the previous day. What we had not expected to find, however, was the high degree of defensive preparation which we now saw. There were Fascist trenches and dug-outs everywhere, all carefully screened with barbed-wire; one of the dug-outs even contained a small, revolving cannon. Many of these fortifications now lay in ruins, pounded almost flat by the shells from the anti-tank guns, and emerging from the rubble were the Fascist defenders who threw their hands in the air and begged for water. For over two days they had been without anything to drink and their first thought was to slake the thirst which was tormenting them so cruelly.

We were extremely proud of our capture of Purburell Hill. It had not been the simple and straightforward exercise that we had initially been led to believe, and had proved, instead, to be one of the most heavily fortified positions that fell to the British Battalion throughout the war. Inevitably,

our losses had been high and many of us who took part in that action could, perhaps, be forgiven for thinking that our task would have been very much easier, and far less costly, had we been provided with adequate air and artillery support with which to pound the Fascist trenches and dug-outs, before ever we set off on that mad scamper up the rocky slopes of Purburell Hill.

While we had been fighting to take Purburell Hill, the Americans of the Lincoln-Washington Battalion had ousted the Fascists from Quinto, and it was to there that we marched from our scene of triumph. To some extent, Quinto was a foretaste of what was to happen at Belchite, although we did not know that at the time. The entire village had been smashed to pieces, and was now nothing more than a dust-covered pile of rubble.

In our initial advance we had bypassed Belchite which still housed a strong Fascist garrison, and it was to there that we in the British Battalion were next despatched. We marched east to the small village of Codo and to our surprise and relief, this had been evacuated by the Fascists who had retreated to the much more heavily fortified village of Belchite itself. After the resistance which we had met at Purburell Hill and Quinto we had expected that Codo would provide a repeat performance but, fortunately we were proved wrong. At Codo came orders changing our line of march. No longer were we to proceed directly to Belchite but, instead, we were sent to Mediana which lay some ten miles to the north of Belchite on the road to Zaragoza. It was important that the Fascists were not allowed free rein there because any enemy force seeking to relieve the garrison trapped in Belchite would have to pass through Mediana. As luck would have it, we ran almost head on into a Fascist convoy which had been sent to relieve Belchite. The fighting at Mediana was short and sharp, and we were able to inflict heavy casualties on the Nationalist troops before they were forced to fall back on Mediana. Now that we knew that the besieged Belchite garrison would remain so for a while, the British Battalion was drawn up in a cordon overlooking Mediana lest another attempt to relieve Belchite be made later. Within a few days the Lincolns, with support from units of the British Battalion, had fought their way into Belchite. Using grenades and petrol bombs the Republican forces slowly drove the Fascists from house to house in the narrow streets of the village. The Fascists finally surrendered on 6th September but only after some of the bloodiest fighting that I ever saw in Spain in which no quarter was given by either side.

With Quinto and Belchite in Republican hands, if in less than pristine condition, the British Battalion was pulled out of the front line, and placed

in a reserve position for ten days. I can rarely recall being so much in need of a few days' peace and quiet. As an *Enlace* attached to Battalion Headquarters I reckoned that I had run over half of Aragon since the start of the campaign! While being a messenger gave me the advantage of knowing more about what was going on than the average infantryman could ever hope to, it did have its disadvantages. Always I seemed to be going backwards and forwards as fast as my legs would carry me and, almost inevitably, I was busiest when things were most perilous. How I survived unscathed my many excursions up, down and across Purburell Hill, Mediana, Quinto and Belchite, I shall never know. In quieter moments I was tempted to think that the extra knowledge which came my way was bought at an inflated price when set against the risks I took to deliver messages to units pinned down by enemy fire. All too often I seemed to be the one running across exposed land, dodging bullets when others had found a few rocks behind which to shelter. But looking at things rationally, no one is safe on a battlefield and I am certain that everything balanced out overall; for every time I took a chance by moving back and forth from platoon to Battalion Headquarters under fire, I must have been saved on many occasions by moving out of danger to somewhere safer.

Not long after our return to the front, the British Battalion began to advance up the Ebro Valley toward Zaragoza. Our objective was Fuentes de Ebro and if we had taken it we would have been able to see Zaragoza in the distance. With such a prize almost within sight our morale and excitement were quite terrific: we felt that we were at last making significant inroads into Fascist-held territory, as we overcame all of the resistance we encountered. The list of our victories was beginning to lengthen: Purburell Hill, Quinto, Mediana, Belchite. Never before had we advanced so successfully and, inspired by our progress and the nearness of the alluring prize of Zaragoza, our spirits soared and our determination to win hardened still further. This rekindling of optimism must also, at least in part, be attributed to Harold Fry, who had assumed Command of the Battalion. Paddy O'Daire had been sent on an advanced training course for senior officers at Pozorrubio. Harold had been the Machine-Gun Company Commander at Jarama, and it had been the guns under his control which had saved the Battalion during the initial heavy fighting there. At a later stage in that battle, he had been taken prisoner by the Fascists and then exchanged. After a spell back in Britain he had insisted on returning to Spain and we were all glad of his presence.

However, high morale and determination, crucial qualities in any

successful military enterprise, did not guarantee victory, and at Fuentes de Ebro our triumphal progress stopped: Zaragoza was to remain an unattainable goal. For the advance on Fuentes de Ebro, the Brigade structure was altered so that the Canadian Battalion, the MacKenzie-Papineau, replaced the Dimitrov Battalion. Also, for once, an International Brigade Battalion was not employed as the shock force in the assault. The honour of leading the Republican attack fell to the 24th Spanish Battalion. The plan was that the Spanish troops should be carried through and beyond the Fascist front-line positions on the tops of our tanks and then drop from their vehicles and attack the enemy from the rear, whilst the rest of the Brigade advanced in support. Such a venture had a high degree of audacity, which often brings success but also calls for a high degree of preparatory training and discipline. The relatively inexperienced soldiers of the 24th had had no opportunity to acquire these however. The attack went badly wrong for a host of reasons, and Fuentes de Ebro remained in Fascist hands. Sadly our new Commanding Officer, Harold Fry, was killed in the fighting. Fuentes de Ebro never did fall to us and, at the end of October, the Aragon Front stabilized, and the British Battalion was pulled out of line and sent back to Quinto.

Within a fortnight of our return, I was drafted to Tarazona de la Mancha to be trained as an officer.

I took with me many memories of that campaign on the journey south, memories that have stayed with me over the intervening years and, thanks to the tricks which memory plays, have seemed to grow more vivid rather than fade with time. I shall always remember the savagery of the fighting, especially the street fighting, and storming the heavily fortified defences, and the climate. The British Battalion had gained some experience of street fighting at Villanueva de la Canada in the previous July when it had fought its way into the outskirts of the village. I am not ashamed to admit that I was not keen on this aspect of warfare, simply because it is so treacherous. You kick open a door with no knowledge of what is waiting for you on the other side. It could be a bunch of kiddies, it could be a man with a gun, or it could equally well be both. You had to be extremely careful what you were shooting at and when, and never more so than when you knew for certain that there were civilians trapped in the buildings. Although such fighting is an inevitable part of war, it is war at its most grotesque, and it is not something that I would, or did, do from choice. Give me a nice open field any day where you know where everybody is and there is little doubt in your mind as to what you are about. The fortified defences held by the Fascists were an obstacle that we had not previously

83

encountered on such a scale, but again, there were anomalies, and at some places on the front they were totally absent and there was little to suggest that a war was being fought. I recall that one day a small group under the direction of our much famed Quartermaster, Hookey Walker, went by lorry to a staunchly Anarchist village where there was reputed to be a good stock of wine. Hookey was a master scrounger and wheeler- dealer, qualities that are prerequisites for all successful quartermasters in armies the world over, and while he bartered with the local mayor, trying to exchange cigarettes for wine, since money had long since lost its appeal, I walked to the edge of the village where there was a large circular sign on which was written '*Peligroso el Frente*', 'Danger Front Line'. There was no barricade, no barbed wire, and no troops to be seen, just that rather incongruous sign and beyond it a road, cultivated fields, and in the distance, another village which I knew to be in Fascist hands. I was left to wonder how much of the carefully tended fields belonged to each of the ideologically opposed villages, and was left with the suspicion that in the practical, down-to-earth way of peasants everywhere, these two villages had reached an agreement that they would leave each other alone to lead their own lives in their own way as long as neither made any threatening move toward the other. Finally, I shall always remember the weather, which changed quite remarkably during the fighting in Aragon. After days of blazing heat we were subjected to terrific thunderstorms with no real prospect of gaining shelter from the torrential rain which accompanied them. One evening, with the land brilliantly lit by sheets of continuous lightning, I took shelter under an isolated tree. I had my rifle, with bayonet attached, hanging over my shoulder, and I was leaning on an entrenching tool feeling far from happy with my soaking wet uniform, clinging to me like a second skin, when the tree under which I was standing was struck by lightning. The tree split in half and I was thrown several yards. If the lightning had struck any closer I would have been killed outright; as it was, I was simply deafened for a few hours and bruised from the heavy landing which terminated my impromptu flight through the air. Another example of Gregory's luck!

Looking back on the Aragon Campaign I feel that the British Battalion, and indeed all of the Republican units which were involved in it, fought remarkably well. We did score a number of victories against a well-prepared and resolute enemy and our morale was never dampened by the setbacks we encountered, the inhospitable terrain and the vagaries of the weather. However, perhaps we could have done better than we actually did. Perhaps we should have taken Zaragoza, but its capture always

eluded us, even though at times it was so tantalizingly close that our forward units could see its lights twinkling further up the Ebro Valley in the dark of night. Perhaps if we had possessed a leadership with just a little more tactical experience, perhaps if our training and equipment had been just a little better, perhaps if our communications had been just that little more efficient, perhaps if we had enjoyed better air and artillery support, perhaps . . . but the list can go on endlessly. It is always easy to speculate and be wise after the event, especially from the comfort of an armchair far removed from the heat of battle. 'Perhaps' is a luxury which belongs more to historians benefiting from hindsight than to men fighting at the front.

* * *

The Battle of Brunete, which had lasted three weeks, was one of the most brutal and vicious encounters of the war. The battle-hardened shock troops of the Republican Army suffered over 25,000 casualties. This tragic loss of manpower was compounded by the destruction of a significant number of the Republican Army's highly-prized Soviet-supplied tanks and aircraft which were almost impossible to replace. By 26th July 1937 the inroads secured by the initial assault of the Republican forces had been almost entirely surrendered in the face of an extensive Nationalist counter-attack. Not only had the Republic failed in its attempt to lift the Nationalist siege of Madrid but, in addition, Franco had repelled the assault without significantly weakening the northern army moving against Santander.

After the success at Guadalajara the failure of a force which had initially outnumbered its opponent in terms of men, guns, tanks and aircraft once again called into question the efficiency of the Republican military machine. The battle plan, which envisaged the capture of Brunete within hours of the opening of the assault, was wildly over-optimistic. The Republic High Command, schooled in the French and Soviet tradition of massed infantry attacks, had completely under-estimated the defensive potential of the fortified Nationalist villages in the path of the assault. Infantry attacks upon these strongholds were at times virtually suicidal while the use of Soviet tanks in the role of artillery support completely ignored their potential to launch a blitzkrieg-style assault through the National-ist lines.

The battle of Brunete also witnessed the unveiling by the

Nationalist Army of its newly acquired military hardware. The arrival of the German eighty-eight millimetre gun and the Messerschmitt 109 proved a decisive turning-point in the battle and possibly also in the course of the war. The 'Eighty-Eight' was an effective match for the Soviet tanks while the ME 109 quickly ended Republican dominance in the air. By the second week of the campaign the Nationalist airforce, despite its numerical inferiority, controlled the skies, and used its fire-power to devastating effect against the enemy infantry which was harassed at every turn. Despite these problems the Republican Army performed heroic-ally under the most extreme pressure. Only one unit, the XIII International Brigade, cracked, and had to be withdrawn from the line and then only after sustaining appalling losses. It could be contended, however, that the battle tore the heart out of the Republican Army. Although morale was to remain high, even to the bitter end, in strategic terms the Republic committed to battle at Brunete the most seasoned and well-equipped fighting force that it was able to assemble at any point during the war. The failure to achieve a major breakthrough at a time when the military pendulum appeared to be swinging inexorably towards the Nationalists in terms of both numbers and equipment was possibly the turning-point of the war.

The campaign launched in Aragon on 24th August 1937 had sought to remedy some of the errors committed at Brunete. For the first time tanks were deployed in large fast-moving formations seeking to punch holes in the Nationalist front, in an operation which abandoned the previous concentration of resources on a narrow front, in favour of a wide sweeping pincer movement designed to capture Zaragoza. Yet it was quickly apparent that the lessons of Brunete had not been fully absorbed. The defensive capabilities of prepared strongholds were once again sadly under-estimated and, in particular, the town of Belchite which should have been secured on the first day of the operation did not fall until after fifteen days of bitter street fighting. In addition, the political rivalry and confusion surrounding the relative roles of the Army High Command, its Soviet advisers and the political commissars, which had hindered the direction of operations at Brunete, was exacerbated during the course of the Aragon campaign by the hostility generated between the various Communist and Anarchist units employed by the Republican Army.

Within weeks the offensive had ground to a halt and once again the Republic had incurred extensive losses for the gain of little more than a narrow fifteen-mile salient in the Nationalist lines. More seriously, the campaign failed to deflect Nationalist units from the northern front and with the capture of Gijón, on 21st October 1937, Franco eliminated the last vestiges of organized resistance in the north. The fall of the northern provinces not only represented the destruction of a large section of the Republican Army but also secured the industrial capacity of the region, which effectively doubled the production of war material in Nationalist-controlled territory. By November 1937 Franco held two-thirds of Spain and, with the freeing of troops from the

Spain October 1937

northern campaign, it was evident that it would not be long before he threw his forces against the large Republican enclave in eastern Spain.

For the British Battalion the latter half of 1937 was a torrid and testing period. After nineteen days in the line at Brunete the Battalion strength had been reduced from 300 to 42, and of these only 24 were fit for combat. In the following three weeks the Battalion was rapidly rebuilt until it was 400 strong, although this could only be achieved by the dilution of the British contingent with the introduction of 200 Spanish volunteers. Although the Battalion was to retain its distinctive national flavour throughout its term of service in Spain, its formal integration into the Republican Army in September 1937 and the increasing proportion of Spaniards within its ranks were indicative of the appalling losses sustained in its role as one of the key assault forces within the Republican Army.

It was a tribute to the morale of the Battalion and the efficiency of its officers that by the last week of August it was ready to take a full and active part in the Aragon campaign. Once again the British were deployed in the van of the assault and during the course of fierce and protracted street fighting in Belchite the Battalion suffered casualties of approximately seventy-five per cent of its original combat strength. Although again the Battalion was laboriously rebuilt, by November 1937 the British contingent was effectively only one-quarter of the total number. Within the space of little more than ten months the Battalion had seen action at Jarama, Brunete and Belchite and had gained a reputation for dependability and courage. Yet of the men who had marched with such optimism and cheer to the heights of Pingarrón in January 1937 only a handful remained, all of whom had now graduated with alarming speed to the category of war veteran.

4

'Teniente Gregorio': the training school at Tarazona

It was with some trepidation that I journeyed south from Aragon to Tarazona de la Mancha. Never for a moment had I thought that I might one day be asked, and expected, to act as a leader rather than a follower. After all I had never had any prolonged military training, just the small amount I had received at Aldershot and the few weeks at Madrigueras. Admittedly I now had a practical knowledge of warfare and knew what to expect in battle, and I felt that I could help others benefit from my own experiences. Being an officer, however, was something else again. It obviously required qualities of leadership and an ability to motivate others which I had never previously been called upon to display. If I did possess the necessary attributes of an effective and efficient officer then I could not think of a single instance in my life up until then when I had been called upon to exhibit them. Indeed, I very much doubted if I was 'officer material'; the pattern of working-class life in Britain between the wars had done little to inculcate leadership skills. Yet here I was on my way to be trained as a lieutenant, to be made responsible for the actions of others and accountable for the onerous decisions which I would surely have to take. I harboured a deep feeling of anxiety.

The training school at Tarazona was grouped in a number of large houses which had previously belonged to Nationalist sympathizers who had either fled, were in Republican gaols, or had been shot. Although no one was billeted under canvas our accommodation was not luxurious and far too small for the number of troops it had to shelter. Every available space was filled with men and equipment but, despite the inconvenience that this caused, everyone seemed ready to make the most of things and none of the irritability which seems to arise when people are forced to live together in very cramped conditions lasted for long.

For the next few months I worked under Major Merriman, the Commanding Officer at Tarazona. The Major was yet another of those amazing characters who went to Spain to assist the Republic during the

war. He was a stern disciplinarian who missed nothing and would never tolerate any slackness. He was always referred to as 'Major' and never called Bob, not even behind his back, nor was he, to my knowledge, ever the subject of criticism. Over forty years later I met a party of American ex-Spanish Civil War veterans in Madrid who had served with the Lincoln-Washington Battalion and, naturally, I asked if any of them had served with Major Merriman. Their reply did not surprise me. 'Merriman? Oh you mean that West Point guy. Sure we were with him.' The Major was widely understood to have joined the International Brigades direct from the American forces, but he had never been a professional soldier. It was a credit to his self-imposed discipline that he was assumed to have been trained at the US Army's premier military academy when in fact he was an academic from the Universities of Nevada and California. It was dreadfully unfortunate that he was killed in the second battle around Belchite at the beginning of the great Fascist breakthrough to the Mediterranean at Viñaroz in the spring of 1938. The Americans sent many remarkable men to Spain but none of them could rival Major Merriman.

The officer training course was under the direction of an Englishman, Arthur Ollerenshaw, who had served as Second-in-Command of the British Battalion when Paddy O'Daire had taken over its leadership during the recent Aragon Campaign. Because I was the only member of the British Battalion on the course at that time, I was very pleased to see Arthur's familiar face among those of so many strangers. I also had the great good fortune to renew my friendship with Jimmie Rutherford, whom I had not seen since Jarama, who had just completed a course similar to one I was about to begin.

Jimmie had been taken prisoner by the Nationalists during the fighting at Jarama, along with Harold Fry, and had a fascinating tale to tell of his exploits. When the Machine-Gun Company was surrounded and forced to surrender on the second day at Jarama those captured were subjected to the customary Fascist brutality. Three of our comrades, Phil Elias, John Stevens and Ted Dickinson, were shot on the spot as though to emphasize that the Geneva Convention did not extend to Spain. The rest, Jimmie included, were searched and then transported by lorry to prison in Navalcarnero where they were interrogated over seven or eight days by the son of the former Spanish Ambassador to the Court of St James, Merry del Val. By chance they were seen and photographed by a reporter from the *Daily Mail*, not normally a paper noted for its concern for those of a left-wing persuasion. Fortunately for those who had been captured,

the photograph aroused such public interest back in England that they were saved from summary execution. Instead, after long days of brutal questioning, the shaving of their heads and finger-printing, the small band of prisoners was sent to Talavera where it was confined in an old factory because the prison was already bursting at the seams with Spanish Republican sympathizers. For the next three months the captives were to endure a harsh régime of forced labour, meagre diet, no privileges and the constant threat of execution, before being moved on to Salamanca for trial by a military court. They were charged with 'aiding a military rebellion', and the fatuous nature of that indictment was to be indicative of the mockery which the trial assumed. Five of the prisoners, including Harold and Jimmie, were sentenced to death while the remainder received twenty-year sentences. Their fates having been pronounced, the prisoners were confined in the Model Prison in Salamanca along with 5,000 civilians, in accommodation built to house 250. As Jimmie said, 'Those figures say everything for the standard of comfort we enjoyed in Salamanca'.

Despite the impending threat of execution and continuing imprisonment, those enduring the privations of life in Nationalist captivity kept their spirits high by all sorts of means, and their resilience was rewarded in May 1937 when twenty-three of them were exchanged for Fascist officers who had fallen into Republican hands. After being allowed to bathe for the first time since they had been captured, they were transported to the French frontier at the beginning of their journey back to Britain. Barely had they reached England before Harold and Jimmie and a few others insisted on being sent back to Spain to rejoin the Battalion, and within six weeks they were being accorded a heart-felt welcome 'home' by their comrades at the front.

Such resolution speaks volumes for their courage and tenacity and, with men such as those in our ranks, it is not surprising that our morale was never allowed to flag for long. They set a standard of dedication and commitment that the rest of us could only marvel at and strive to emulate, but which we knew we could never hope to exceed.

I wish I could say that Jimmie returned safely from Spain but, alas, he did not. There are all too few happy endings in war. When, on 21st March 1938, the British Battalion ran foul of an Italian armoured column near Calaceite, Jimmie was again taken prisoner and interned in Zaragoza. Again he was interrogated and, as ill-luck would have it, the interrogator was none other than the same Merry del Val who had interrogated him after his capture at Jarama. Val recognized Jimmie almost at first glance

and Jimmie was sentenced to death and executed, thus paying the price of twice falling into Fascist hands. Jimmie's courage should have earned him a nobler end; but there was little that was noble about the fighting in Spain, although some men managed to maintain a special kind of dignity and humanity in the face of even the greatest barbarity: Jimmie was one of that remarkable breed. I could mention many others equally deserving of admiration.

Even though the cramped conditions at Tarazona meant that it was not an ideal situation in which to undergo training, I had no complaints whatsoever about the content or quality of the instruction I received. It highlighted my naïveté about virtually all things of a military nature! It is all too easy to find examples of my lack of knowledge. When I first arrived at the training centre I had little conception of the tactics of warfare, despite my experience of battlefield conditions. For instance, I assumed that on sighting the enemy you strung your men out into a line and put a machine-gun here and there at what looked like an appropriate place and resolved to give your opponents hell if they had the audacity to try to break through. I had never really appreciated the importance of organizing a front in depth, of ensuring that, if the front-line men were slaughtered or captured, then the attacking forces should be confronted by another defensive position which had been prepared in advance of their attack; that machine-guns should not be simply slotted haphazardly into the front-line but situated to the rear to avoid them being captured or smashed by the first artillery barrage, and that they should be sited so as to have an open field of fire at the enemy, if necessary, over the heads of one's troops. I was astounded by my ignorance.

I also learned to fire a machine-gun for the first time, having previously placed reliance on a rifle. The gunnery course was especially thorough. For example, knowing how to fire and reload a machine-gun properly was not enough: I also had to learn how to strip it down completely and how to reassemble it in the dark. I spent many frustrating hours wearing a blindfold while striving to slot the various parts of a Maxim together. Some of my early efforts bore a striking resemblance to the drawings of Heath Robinson, but eventually I could complete the tricky exercise almost in my sleep.

Although the Soviet Union provided most of the arms and ammunition used by the Republican forces, Soviet nationals were very thin on the ground. Certainly, Soviet military advisers did operate in Spain and occasionally appeared at Brigade and Battalion headquarters, but the only one with whom I ever had the opportunity to talk was based at the training

school at Tarazona. Like all of the Russians in Spain he did not use his real name but went under the pseudonym of Ramón. After a few drinks 'Ramón' became 'Ramonski' but I never did learn his true identity. He spoke neither Spanish nor English but several of the Americans at Tarazona had relatives who had been refugees from either Tsarist or Soviet Russia and these comrades had been brought up speaking Russian as their native tongue and acted as interpreters. Ramón gave away little of his past and present activities even when he had consumed large measures of heady Spanish wine. All that we really came to know of Ramón was that he was a veteran of the Russian Revolution and the civil war which followed in its wake, and that he was an adviser on training methods. No doubt much of his hard-earned experience had been incorporated into the training course which I underwent.

My course at Tarazona finished shortly before Christmas 1937 and, having satisfied my instructors, I became an acting lieutenant, a *teniente*. My second Christmas in Spain was no different from the first: Christmas did not impinge on my activities. I am sure that people back home in England had been collecting together little luxuries like cigarettes, chocolate and soap to send to Spain, but no parcels or cards reached Tarazona. As the mail service was atrocious at the best of times, I was hardly surprised that no news and seasonal greetings were forthcoming from my family and friends. In the predominantly Anarchist villages in which we were based, Christmas was a great non-event, as the locals were totally caught up in their anti-clerical convictions and we did not feel it right or proper to offend their sensitivities by seeking to organize any of the festivities of an English Christmas, such as a celebratory drink or a special meal, even if we could have produced them from the limited range of provisions in the Quartermaster's store! So Christmas 1937 was as bleak of festive bonhomie as had been Christmas 1936. The cookhouse at Tarazona made no effort to extend its menu, but simply served up the same inevitable diet of beans and rice. Nor was there any break in the pattern of our daily routine: it was just another day of drill and exercises.

If there was a disappointing similarity between my first two Christmases in Spain I had changed quite remarkably as a person. Like so many of those who had volunteered to go to fight for the Republic, I had developed strong leanings toward Anarchism and a fraternal bond with its advocates. Their obvious sincerity, dedication and enthusiasm were wonderful to see. No amount of hardship seemed to lessen their deeply held conviction in the natural justice of their cause or the inevitability of its fulfilment. Of course, reflecting back on it now, from a distance of nearly

fifty years, I can see that the hopes which the Anarchists entertained were simply dreams lacking in practicality, but at the time I felt quite differently about things. When I had first arrived in Spain my determination to play a part in the crushing of Fascism had been strong and it remained undiminished. If anything, I was now more firmly resolved than ever to see this evil creed swept from the face of the earth. I had seen it in action, I had seen during the Brunete campaign the depths of inhumanity to which its advocates would sink to further their ends, and I felt nothing but an overriding contempt for them and a hatred of all that they stood for. Perhaps it was this loathing and a readiness to have a go at the Fascists at each and every opportunity which made me pleased with the way the war was progressing and led me to think that we were on the verge of crushing the Nationalists. Admittedly we had not yet defeated them, but, after a year's fighting, and despite our losses, our morale was still extremely high and I thought it was only a matter of time before we triumphed and I would be on my way home.

I never considered trying to put a date to my departure from Spain and I certainly did not realize that it would be more than twelve months before I next set foot on English soil. Nor did I have any idea of the hardships which I would have to endure before that day arrived. Yet even had I been told that many months would pass before I would be reunited with my family and even had I been informed of the dangers and privations which still awaited me, I feel sure that it would have made not one iota of difference. I was pledged to stay in Spain until the Republic was safe. Such homesickness as I had experienced in the first few weeks had long been forgotten. I enjoyed the companionship of my friends and the constant struggle: the cost of victory was well worth the price we were paying. I saw myself as having been transformed by my experiences into a professional revolutionary, and was content to think that I was playing my part in changing the world and ridding it of the misery of Fascism. I was quite happy with my lot and had no desire to change it in any shape or form. Spain was the place where the battle against Fascism was being fought, I was a part of that fight, and I wanted neither to do anything else nor be anywhere else. Destiny had drawn me to Spain and there I would stay until the fight was won.

With my own training now completed I was ordered to stay on at Tarazona and assume responsibility for the training of a new group of recruits. Again I had some doubts as to my suitability for such a task but I enjoyed my new work. The recruits for whom I was responsible were of many nationalities. By far the greatest number were Spanish with just a

few from Britain and other European countries. After a little over twelve months in Spain I had acquired a rudimentary working knowledge of the language and was able to drill my new charges in passable Spanish. The Spanish lads were simple peasants. Few of them had been to school, or if they had ever sat in a classroom had not gained much from the experience! When it came to pay day, they simply had to place a thumb-print on the army pay sheet to show that they had received their ten pesetas a day. They were, however, as good a bunch of young men as you could ever hope to meet and I got along with them extremely well.

Every morning we made an early start and I would race them to the local brook for half an hour of horse-play before we settled down to the real work of drill. The first time I took my youthful charges on to the firing ranges was a bit of an eye-opener for me. Most of the recruits had never seen, let alone held, a rifle before. The rather ferocious recoil of the standard issue Soviet-made rifle did little to overcome their obvious trepidation, but worse was to follow a few days later when I began to instruct them in the use of a hand-grenade. Having held up the grenade for their inspection, I removed the pin and grasping the grenade tightly I began to move among the assembled ranks to show them how safe it was. I explained that, if properly held, even an armed grenade can do no harm; you could sit down and eat your dinner if you wanted to with one in your hand with no fear of being blown to pieces, as long as you do not loosen your grip on it. My young Spanish recruits were unconvinced about the accuracy of the information which I was imparting, and as soon as they realized that I was demonstrating with a live grenade they threw themselves behind the nearest sandbags with their arms raised to protect their heads, knees drawn up to their stomachs, and their eyes tightly closed!

Gradually, however, their confidence and abilities improved, and at the end of the two-month training period they had assumed a more than passable military bearing which, given my lack of experience as an instructor and their previous dearth of knowledge of all things military, was probably all that could be achieved. Certainly they could have benefited from a more prolonged training, but events at the front ruled out that possibility, for with the arrival of New Year came news of heavy fighting at Teruel.

Now for the one and only time while I was in Spain I began to resent what I was being asked to do. I was in the safety of Tarazona with a relatively cushy job, while my own Battalion was fighting at Teruel. I felt that my place was with my comrades at the front; after all, I had been with

them in every engagement so far and felt that I should be with them now. My resentment at being 'confined' so far from the action increased still further when I learned of the death of one of my close friends from Nottingham, Bernard Winfield, during the fighting at Teruel. I had known Bernard for several years, indeed almost from the first day I had gone to live in Nottingham after leaving Lincoln. His death came as a bitter blow to me; the one which caused me the greatest anguish and deepest sense of loss that I experienced in Spain. He was one of the pleasantest and most sincere people that anyone could ever wish to meet. He was killed on 20th January in the ferocious fighting which developed as the British Battalion sought to stem the Fascist attack which had been directed against its position on the approach to Teruel. I immediately went to see Major Merriman and asked to be sent back to my battalion. My request was turned down and he told me that he had a desire, every bit as strong as my own, to rejoin the Lincoln-Washingtons, but he had been given strict instructions to remain in his present posting, and I was to do likewise. I tried to get Major Merriman's decision reversed by taking my case to the Political Department, but to no avail. So the early part of 1938 found me carrying on with the training of the new recruits and itching all the time to get back to my friends and comrades in the north.

Eventually, in February, I was released and sent to rejoin my battalion which was by this time in a rest position near Lecera, having withdrawn from the Teruel front. Accompanying me on the journey to Aragon were about 200 recruits, both Spanish and English, many of whom I had trained at Tarazona, and who were now to fill the gaps left in the Battalion's ranks by the recent losses in battle and through sickness. I just hoped that the newcomers had been sufficiently well-schooled to take their places alongside the veteran campaigners whose hardships they would now be sharing.

With this new influx of Spanish lads the composition of the Battalion had undergone a profound change. When a year earlier the British Battalion had been formed and when it had first gone into battle at Jarama its ranks had been exclusively filled with British volunteers. The severe fighting of the intervening twelve months and the difficulty of getting British volunteers into Spain meant that such a situation could no longer be sustained. By the end of February 1938 roughly half the men in its ranks were Spanish nationals with an experienced core of British old-timers. This was a development which I welcomed as I had always felt that it had been a mistake to constitute 'national' battalions, and I had long argued that 'mixed' battalions with a strong Spanish input would have

helped to develop a sense of identity with the cause for which both we overseas volunteers and the native Spanish Republicans were fighting. This, of course, had happened, but it had done so by chance: a fact that highlighted the casual approach to matters which all too often was the order of the day on the Republican side in Spain. If I held a reservation, it was that the Battalion had only one Spanish officer. This was explained by the fact that few of our Spanish comrades had either the education or experience to enable them to hold positions of authority. So many of the young Spanish lads could not read or write, and this made it impossible for them to be promoted. Others of our Spanish complement had been regular soldiers in the Spanish Army before the Insurrection, and some of them had seen combat in North Africa, but none of them had held a commission. Many from this latter group did become sergeants and corporals with the British Battalion and conducted themselves most ably. One point which must be made is that all of the Spaniards serving with the British Battalion were volunteers like ourselves; they did not have to serve with us. They did so from choice and in the knowledge that they were joining troops who had been used consistently to spearhead attacks, and so would always be thrown into the most perilous situation. They knew that by serving with the Battalion they were not going to be assigned patrol duties on a quiet sector of the front, but instead would be in the thick of the fighting. Many of them may have been illiterate and most of them may have been devoid of any previous military training before throwing in their lot with us, but their courage and fortitude more than compensated for those shortcomings.

I was now a *teniente* in charge of one of the Battalion's four companies, in command of 150 men divided into three sections. The training I had received at Tarazona, the experience of training raw troops and the vast number of new responsibilities which I now had to assume meant that the anxiety which I had felt when travelling to join the officers' course a few months previously was a thing of the past and had been replaced by a sense of excitement and a desire to prove my metal as a leader.

Bill Alexander, who had commanded the British Battalion at Teruel, had been replaced by Sam Wild. Bill's wounds received at Teruel had not responded to medical treatment and so he was sent back to England. For a week or two we were frantically busy re-equipping and continuing the training of our new Spanish comrades, while others held the front line in Aragon. However, on 9th March, our preparations were brought to a sudden end, the Fascists had launched a massive offensive against our forces. The attack began with an intense artillery bombardment and air

97

attacks of such severity that the Republican troops were forced to give ground and the battalions of the International Brigade were rushed to the front to stem the Fascist onslaught. Clearly we were in for a very rough ride and I was about to find out just how much I had managed to digest of the training course at Tarazona and what sort of a fist I had made of the training of our new batch of recruits.

* * *

In contrast to the growing unity and discipline stamped by the Nationalist forces on their zone of occupation, the Republican administration was continually hampered by thinly veiled hostility between the various factions within the Popular Front. Assassination and persecution of political rivals were commonplace as the various Anarchist, Communist and Socialist factions manoeuvred for position. In general the Spanish Communist Party held the ascendancy, largely due to the rigid chain of command and discipline it imposed upon its members, which gave it an inherent advantage over its competitors and marked it as a symbol of stability in the whirlpool of Spanish politics. Furthermore, the party was given immense leverage by the fact that the Republic was heavily dependent on the flow of arms and advisers from the Soviet Union. The power of the party was indicated clearly in May 1937 when it led a political coalition which unseated the Prime Minister, Largo Caballero. Hailed as 'the Spanish Lenin', Caballero had enjoyed immense popular prestige but his determination to resist the suppression of the anti-Stalinist factions in Catalonia and his attempt to curb the power of the Communist-dominated political commissars alienated him from the Communist Party and ultimately sealed his fate.

Caballero's successor, Juan Negrín, faced a monumental task in attempting to revive the flagging fortunes of the Republic. Following the stalemate at Brunete and the fall of Asturias, the most pressing problem was to seize the initiative from the Nationalist Army, particularly as it was known that Franco intended to launch a further assault upon Madrid in the third week of December 1937. In order both to defuse this attack and repair sagging morale it was important that the Republican Army once again went on the offensive. The target selected was Teruel, the provincial capital. Already surrounded by Republican forces on all

but its western approaches and defended by a maximum of 17,000 troops it was anticipated that Teruel could be quickly secured by a mass Republican attack. The offensive opened on 15th December 1937 when General Rojo threw 40,000 out of a total force of approximately 100,000 men against the Nationalist forces. The battle involved some of the fiercest fighting of the war as the Republican Army, in subzero temperatures and falling snow, engaged the Nationalists in bitter street fighting, literally blasting the retreating garrison from successive strongpoints.

Teruel was not finally captured until 8th January 1938. Although the weather took its toll amongst the Republican infantry, in general, it assisted their cause by grounding the Nationalist airforce and immobilizing their lines of communication. By the second half of January, however, the Nationalists had gathered sufficient forces to the west of Teruel to stage a major counterattack. The assault opened on 5th February 1938 when, in the course of a four-day engagement north of the city, the Republican Army suffered a severe reverse and was forced to evacuate the town of Alfambra. Confronted with the prospect of being encircled by the superior fire-power of the advancing Nationalist Army, the defenders of Teruel became increasingly desperate. Amid charge and countercharge of treachery and desertion, the last Communist and Anarchist units were finally forced out of the city on 22nd February 1938. Once again the Republican Army for little or no gain had incurred enormous losses. It was estimated that 14,000 Republican soldiers were killed during the course of the battle and vast amounts of irreplaceable equipment were abandoned during the subsequent retreat from the city. The engagement had indicated that the discipline of the Nationalist Army combined with its overwhelming air and artillery support were too much for the Republican Army. Despite acts of immense heroism by its infantry the Republican Army was essentially outgunned and outfought. In addition, the battle further highlighted the problem of creating an effective military machine when collaboration between various units was often only grudgingly and reluctantly given.

The British Battalion of the XVth International Brigade was only employed in the later stages of the battle for Teruel as the Nationalist counter-attack began to roll back the Republican defence. Even so, Walter Gregory was fortunate to miss this

encounter when, over a period of six weeks, in appalling weather conditions, the battalion fought a series of rearguard actions in an attempt to stem the Nationalist advance. After Teruel the battalion was moved to northern Aragon to meet a Nationalist advance at Segura de los Baños. It was apparent, however, that this was only an opening engagement, as Franco sought to exploit the weakness and disorganization of the Republican forces following the battle of Teruel. By March 1938 the Nationalists had assembled over 100,000 men supported by approximately 600 aircraft and 200 tanks, for an assault designed to push the Republican Army out of Aragon and to break through to the eastern seaboard north of Valencia. If the campaign was successful the Republican zone would be divided into two, isolating Catalonia from the centre of government in Valencia.

5

Retreat from Aragon

Walter rejoined his Battalion in February 1938. When the Nationalist assault was finally launched on 9th March 1938 the British were assigned to defend the town of Belchite. They were confronted by an organized and confident enemy using powerful tank concentrations to punch large holes in the Republican lines to be exploited by infantry with extensive artillery and air support. With only limited artillery and having surrendered the skies to the Nationalist airforce it was quickly apparent that it would be difficult to hold even prepared strongpoints at Belchite, Caspe and Gandesa. Furthermore, if forced to retreat the arid and featureless landscape of Aragon offered the Republican forces little scope for the rapid erection of further defensive lines. Outnumbered and outgunned there was every possibility that, if dislodged from their strongpoints, the Republican Army would be quickly thrown into a headlong retreat.

* * *

Just how hard was the task ahead became clear as we approached the front. Franco was trying to break the Republic's resistance once and for all with a big offensive across the Aragon plateau and on into Catalonia, thus dividing the Republic into two: the Fascists had assembled the greatest military force that the Civil War had witnessed, with some fifteen Nationalist divisions in place, ready for the assault.

The XVth Brigade established its Headquarters in Belchite, which still carried all of the scars of the earlier fighting there. The town looked even more forlorn than when I had last seen it, with no sign of troops or civilians, and with the smell of the dead buried under piles of rubble. But we had little time to survey this scene of devastation before we were moving north along the seemingly interminable straight road towards

Mediana and Fuentes de Ebro. As we marched to the front we came across remnants of units which had crumbled under the pressure of the initial Fascist thrust, and we suddenly became aware that there were no organized Republican troops between us and the heavy concentration of enemy forces. Soon we were under attack from the air and ground, and the lack of any man-made fortifications and a dearth of good natural defensive positions left us with little option but to fall back first to Belchite, and then beyond it.

Although we did not recognize it at the time, we were now at the start of a retreat through Aragon. We were not, however, in headlong flight, nor had fear and panic replaced military discipline. We were not routed nor were we anything like a rabble; rather we were engaged in a systematic withdrawal, covering our line of march at all times against enemy attack. As the Brigade disengaged itself and fell back, its rear would be covered by a battalion situated at some strategically important point such as a road junction or a piece of high land. At every turn we sought to delay the Fascists so that as much material as possible could be saved, and the sick and wounded transported to safety, for they could expect no mercy if they were to fall into the hands of the Nationalists. By using these tactics we were able to delay the fall of Belchite for a full day but our escape from there was made very hazardous by shrapnel and machine-gun fire from the advanced enemy units.

By late evening on 10th March we had established a defensive position astride the road to Lecera to try to delay any attempted breakthrough by tanks and motorized infantry. Although we were repeatedly strafed by Nationalist planes we met little trouble on the ground. Next day, however, the serious nature of our position was brought home to us when Sam Wild, in attempting to locate the Brigade at Lecera, where it was rumoured to have established its headquarters, found the town already in Fascist hands. Silently, we marched eastward to escape the net that the enemy was tightening around us. Orders received from Brigade Staff at Vinaceite now directed us across country to take up position on the Hijar to Alcaniz road in preparation for the defence of Alcaniz.

After three days of ceaseless movement and fighting, this march proved to be one of the worst I had ever experienced. The heat was intense, there was no water, we had little to eat, and were fast approaching exhaustion even before we set out. To add to our misery we were strafed by low-flying aircraft for mile after agonizing mile, which threw the marching column into constant turmoil and tried our patience to breaking-point.

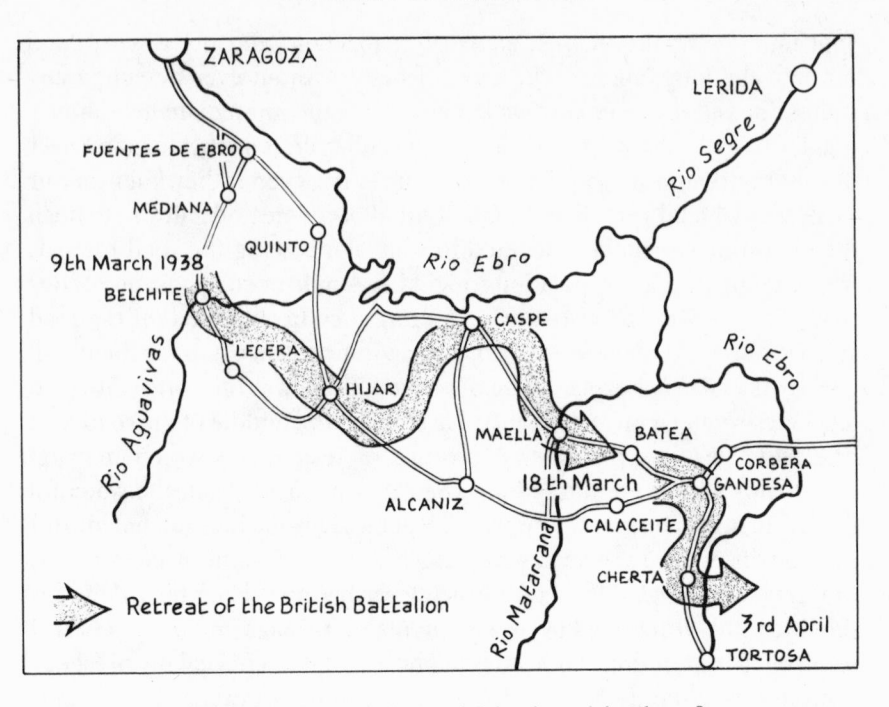

The Retreat from Aragon 9th March–3rd April 1938

Somehow we reached our objective: a hill-top overlooking the Hijar to Alcaniz road and we took up our positions there. Hijar had already fallen to the enemy and after a day in which we were exposed to constant bombardment, we spent the hours of darkness digging into the unyielding ground to gain as much protection as was possible before daylight brought fresh attacks. As the sun rose we realized that our efforts of the night had been futile, for there were no supporting units on our flanks, and the enemy had used the cover of darkness to infiltrate behind our position, thus rendering it untenable. Hastily we pulled out toward Alcaniz under a steady rain of fire from Fascist strong points which dominated the road. Now word reached us that Alcaniz had been taken by Italian units, so again we had to labour across country, this time eastwards towards Caspe. We marched through the day and as evening approached it was the turn of my company to act as rearguard. We had reached an important road junction and I took a section of my company to build a barricade across the road to delay the Fascist advance and give early warning to the main body of our forces of any attacks which might be being prepared. Using whatever materials we could find at hand we set up a crude road-block at a

spot miles from the nearest signs of civilization, and there we waited through the long, cold, dark hours of night without ever detecting any sight or sound of the enemy we knew to be in the immediate neighbour-hood. Occasionally we heard the engines of aircraft as they droned over us, but they had other bigger fish than us to fry, even if they knew of our existence, which I very much doubt. Out of boredom and a desire to push the chill from my limbs I decided to walk alone along the road towards where I thought Fascist positions might be. A mile or so in advance of our road-block, I came to a place where a lorry had been pulled off the road and a group of soldiers were setting up an improvised camp for the night. Clearly they did not expect to be disturbed; there was only one young lad of about seventeen on guard-duty. He stood in the middle of the road with rifle and fixed bayonet in that posture of resignation which men on guard-duty always seem to adopt when they are away from the watchful gaze of an officer and not anticipating trouble. Despite his nonchalant air I was convinced that the sentry had at least caught a sight of me and was simply waiting for me to draw a little closer before raising his rifle to his shoulder and letting me have the contents of its magazine in the chest. I resolved to brazen things out. Making no attempt to conceal my presence I pushed my shoulders back and marched straight towards him in best parade-ground fashion. He did not challenge me. So far so good! I stopped a few inches from him and stared confidently into his face with as haughty an expression as I could muster. I barked at him,

'Which battalion are you from?'

The lad immediately drew himself to attention. So he had not seen me after all. No doubt he had been dreaming of home and the comforts of a warm bed. He told me his battalion and added that his company had just driven from 'Zaragoza, Señor'. If I had any remaining doubts that I had run foul of a Nationalist patrol these were dispelled by his use of the word 'Señor'. Yet our uniforms were sufficiently similar and the night sufficiently dark that it was not possible even at arm's length for him to identify me as his enemy. I wore no badges of rank to distinguish me as a lieutenant (which was customary in the International Brigade), and my confidence and assertiveness alone had made him take me for his superior in his own forces. I knew that any sign of hesitancy, panic or haste on my part would quickly bring the charade to a speedy and unwelcome conclusion, so I casually gazed around me at the camp, gave the young guard a thorough inspection as he remained rigidly at attention, and then calmly began to move back into the shadows at a leisurely pace. I felt a very strong urge to run like mad back to the safety of my section, but resisted

the desire to do so. When I had distanced myself by a few yards from the sentry someone came out of a field behind me and spoke to the lad,

'Who was that?'

'I don't know,' replied the youngster, no doubt surprised at receiving so many visitors in such a short space of time.

'Well why didn't you ask him who he was and what he was about?'

There was no reply to that question that I could hear but I was expecting bullets to come looking for me at any second. I automatically hunched my shoulders and lowered my head until my chin was almost on my chest thus trying to present as small a target as possible and increased my speed from the leisurely amble which I was finding hard to maintain, to the more comforting pace of a very quick march. No bullets came, and as soon as I felt myself to be covered from fire by a dip in the road I ran like the wind toward my section, as the anxiety which I had struggled to suppress burst upon me. The men at the road-block heard my approach and began to pack up immediately, and within minutes we were moving out toward the Battalion.

The Battalion was already beginning the next phase of its withdrawal when we made contact, and I reported my encounter with the Fascist patrol to Sam Wild. He was untroubled by my news and told me that other sections had brought in reports that confirmed that the enemy was on every side of us.

By this stage in our retreat, news that we were again surrounded caused little dismay, as it now seemed to be a regular occurrence, constantly presenting us with the problem of finding the weakest link in the encircling forces, breaking through at that point with all speed before reinforcements could be pitted against us, and then continuing to fall back until such time as the entire process began again. It took us all of the day and well into the night to reach Caspe, which was only some twenty miles to the east of Hijar by road, but we must have covered nearer thirty miles over rough terrain to get there. As we slumped to the ground in the olive groves outside Caspe, it was difficult to think of ourselves as a fighting force. Certainly we were still organized and possessed a proper leadership, but the men were totally spent. It had been at least three days since any of us in my company had slept for even a few minutes. The almost total absence of food and water, the energy-sapping marches across rough country under a ferocious sun, and the constant harassment by the enemy both on the ground and from the air meant that we were completely drained, physically and mentally. Five hundred men had marched through Belchite but I doubt if more than 150 reached Caspe, and not

one of us could have offered even token resistance had we been attacked at that moment. Fortunately we were spared that horror, and a night's sleep and the first food that we had eaten in what seemed like months rather than days worked the customary minor miracle. When we were called upon the next morning to fill our ammunition pouches and move through Caspe to take the heights which the Fascists held to the west of the town, we did so with something resembling our old resolve.

Again we were battered from the air and from artillery assaults before becoming partially encircled by a sustained Fascist infantry attack. Now events grew very confused, and hand-to-hand fighting became the order of the day. I abandoned any attempt to give orders to what remained of my company: it was simply a case of each man for himself. At one point Sam Wild was actually captured along with a small group of comrades, all of whom managed to escape after an old-fashioned free-for-all with their guards. Somehow, and I do not know how even to this day, those of us who were still able to stand and fight formed a defensive cordon on the east side of Caspe to hold the advanced enemy patrols which were working their way forward through the shattered buildings. By nightfall the Fascists had brought tanks into Caspe itself, and we were forced to retreat under intense close-range rifle and machine-gun fire out of the rubble and across country toward Maella. No longer were we organized in battalions, now we were simply the remnants of the XVth Brigade. Few in number, exhausted to the verge of collapse, with but a few rounds of ammunition per man remaining, we waded the next day across the Matarrana river, a tributary of the mighty River Ebro, and reached Batea.

Batea provided us with what we most desperately needed: shelter, food and sleep. And it gave us the chance to reorganize the Brigade. Day after day men wandered into the town either alone or in small groups to be afforded a 'right royal' reception by their comrades who had presumed them dead or captured. That so many men did manage to reach Batea after having lost contact with their units was nothing short of a miracle and says much for their determination. With no provisions, frequently without ammunition, moving by night and hiding by day and with nothing but the most rudimentary of maps to guide them, they had made their way through territory thick with enemy patrols to the safety of the Brigade, and were still prepared to take up where they had left off.

While we rested at Batea the Battalion was brought back to full strength with the return of the wounded from treatment and convalescence and with new arrivals from the training camps in the south. Sam Wild was promoted to Captain in recognition of the crucial role he had played in the

recent fighting and was then promptly despatched to Barcelona for rest and medical treatment. George Fletcher took over command of the Battalion from Sam and Wally Tapsell returned from sick leave to resume his role as Battalion Political Commissar.

We knew the period of tranquillity we were enjoying at Batea was but temporary, and that before long we would once again be called upon to pit our strength against another Fascist onslaught. There was simply no way of escaping the fact that the Nationalist generals were trying to split the Republican forces into two by driving a wedge to the coast in the region of Tortosa, 20 miles south of where we were. On 30th March the anticipated offensive broke against our front at two points: south of the River Ebro and also slightly further to the north along the River Segre and in the vicinity of Lerida. Immediately the XVth Brigade was alerted and moved to the front to bolster other Republican units which were taking the full impact of the new assault.

As I led my company along the road to Gandesa a small aeroplane of the type used by the Fascists for reconnaissance swooped down upon us from out of a cloudless sky. I shouted to my men to take no notice but to smile at the pilot so that he could take some pleasing pictures. No sooner had the ribald remarks which followed my light-hearted instructions finished than we found ourselves being bombed with leaflets. As such a thing had never happened before it gave rise to a good deal of mirth and merriment and another outbreak of wise-cracks. We chased the leaflets as they blew along the dusty ground in the wind but on reading them our laughter disappeared. The content of the message which each leaflet carried was brief, 'Lerida Today, Barcelona Tomorrow'. Lerida? If the Fascists had taken Lerida then I knew that we were hopelessly cut off: our avenue to safety had been removed. Later, of course, I learnt that the Fascist claim to have taken Lerida was untrue, but at the time we all experienced a terrible sinking feeling which was deepened by the other words on the leaflet which read something along the lines of:

Red soldiers, you have been deceived by your leaders. Take this leaflet along with your equipment to the nearest Nationalist forces. Surrender peacefully and you will be treated with justice.

Then came the punch line:

This does not apply to war criminals who will be dealt with severely for the crimes they have perpetrated against the Spanish people.

I can remember thinking, 'Well, Walter my lad, that puts you in your place and no mistake'.

Strangely the call to surrender gradually dispelled the anxiety we had felt on reading the claim that Lerida had fallen. The Spanish boys in the company knew where Lerida was and quickly realized the effect that its capture would have upon us, whereas their English comrades had no idea of the location of the place nor of the significance which it held for us. Why, though, if Lerida was safe in Fascist hands were we being called upon to surrender? With our escape-route blocked, it was only a matter of time before we ended up in either a Nationalist prisoner-of-war camp or against a brick wall. Somehow the message did not ring true. Again I had occasion to admire the young Spanish lads for, never for a moment, did they consider surrendering to the Fascists and securing their own safety, when they realized the fate which awaited their English comrades. Still united, if more than a little shaken, we marched on toward Gandesa and on through it to the small village of Calaceite.

It was intended that the British Battalion should take up position in support of, and in reserve to, the crack Communist 11th Division led by Enrique Lister. The front was in a state of turmoil and we received a very thorough working over by Fascist artillery. Yet it was imperative that we checked the enemy advance to permit other Republican forces to retreat to Catalonia through the mountains. What was not known either by Brigade or Battalion staff as we moved forward was that the Listers had already retreated even as we approached the front and that we were about to receive the full force of the Fascist advance in that sector. As we turned a bend in the road we ran foul of a column of enemy light tanks which were bound for Calaceite. Another group of tanks broke cover from a wood on our flank and Italian infantry in large numbers entered the fray in support of their armour. All hell broke loose as enemy tanks and infantry poured fire into the leading companies of the Battalion and as soon as the order was given to scatter and make for the hills we broke into ones and twos and sought cover wherever we could find it. Fortunately our Machine-Gun Company, which had been at the rear of the Battalion, was able to secure some high ground and bring its guns quickly into action, thus affording crucial covering fire while those of us on the road sought to disengage ourselves from the fighting and make good our escape.

It was in the chaos and slaughter of this engagement that Wally Tapsell, surely the greatest of all of those who served as political commissars in Spain, was last seen firing at the enemy tanks. So fierce was the fighting

that we had no opportunity to gather together our wounded and take them with us; Wally, along with all too many others, had to be left where he fell. I would like to think that Wally died in battle before the Fascists found him, for assuredly he would have been subjected to barbaric treatment before being executed had he been taken alive. Wally was a great colleague. He was a Cockney through and through and saw humour in every situation. A few days earlier I had remarked to him that I was badly in need of a haircut. Wally assured me that he was the very man to carry out that exercise and that I had no need to look further for a trained trimmer of hair. From a first-aid kit he extracted a small pair of scissors and armed with these he began to cut my hair by using the simple device of grabbing chunks of unruly locks in his left hand and hacking away at them with the minuscule and blunt scissors. My new appearance aroused both concern and amusement, but certainly not even the faintest sign of envy. I lost count of the number of times I had conversations over the next few days which began,

'What's happened to you? Are you all right?'

'Yes thanks I'm fine. I've had a haircut.'

'I can see that. Who did it?'

'Wally Tapsell.'

'My God. I hope he didn't charge you.'

I shall always remember Wally, not only for the sterling service he gave the Battalion, but also for the haircut.

Those of us who survived the first Fascist onslaught now had to make our way back to the rear through country swarming with enemy troops. I tried to regroup my company but this proved impossible for my men, far outnumbered, were now spread far and wide as they sought to escape from the vastly superior enemy formations which were still pressing home their advance and busily capitalizing on their initial successes. Eventually I did manage to bring together a couple of dozen men but they were drawn from several companies and I was never again to see many of those whom I had led through Gandesa and Calaceite a few hours earlier.

Now that I had lost contact with Battalion Headquarters, I considered it too great a risk to start searching for it in the disarray which threatened to overwhelm us. I opted to lead my small party back to Calaceite – only to find that it was occupied by enemy troops. I could see no other course of action but to skirt round the village and make for Gandesa across country, but always keeping within striking distance of the road, as I felt sure that if the Brigade had managed to establish some sort of order out of the chaos, then they would attempt to check the Fascist advance before it could burst

upon Gandesa. At the point where the minor road from Batea fed into the Calaceite-Gandesa road we made contact with a group of about sixty members of the Battalion who had decided to make a stand. Malcolm Dunbar, Brigade Chief of Staff, who had moved up to the front with the British Battalion, had assumed command of this motley collection of survivors and at dawn on 2nd April we cautiously worked our way around Gandesa and took up position a short distance to the south-east of the town at a point where the Gandesa-Tortosa road ran through a cutting, flanked by a steep-sided ridge. This was an ideal defensive position because it would have proved unacceptably costly to the enemy to attempt to force it by a frontal assault and was, at the same time, extremely difficult to outflank. From there we sent out patrols to try to locate the Fascist's advanced units and to provide early warning of any attacking build-up. Until late in the morning there were few indications of a threat to our position emerging and by midday our patrols had managed to bring in numerous groups of Republican stragglers, so that our small force grew in size until there were almost 200 drawn from a variety of XVth Brigade Battalions: Spanish, British, Canadian, American and a few Germans from the Thaelmann Battalion of the XI Brigade. A light tank with a Spanish crew also appeared from our rear and was positioned astride the road in the middle of the cutting thus adding considerably to the strength of the resistance that we would be able to offer when the enemy attacked.

In the early afternoon the inevitable Fascist assault began, but it lacked much of the effect that it might otherwise have had, because low cloud precluded air strikes against our position and because the speed of the enemy advance had not permitted him the time to bring his heavy artillery up to the front line. We successfully repulsed the Nationalists' leading cavalry patrols with little difficulty and an infantry attack which took place early in the afternoon was a rather half-hearted affair and posed no real threat. Our machine-guns halted an armoured car patrol and set one of the vehicles ablaze. Despite the constant harassment we endured our casualties were few because of the protection given by the terrain. As dusk drew in the enemy advance was still halted in the valley below us and Malcolm Dunbar decided that our delaying task was almost complete and that the time had come for the bulk of our force to fall back and continue the retreat through the mountains into Catalonia. To prevent the Fascists realizing that the road ahead of them lay open – and hence presented them with the opportunity to fall upon the retreating troops – Dunbar detailed me to take up position on the north side of the road and hold the pass for as long as I felt possible before making a speedy withdrawal.

A dozen volunteers placed themselves under my command and we began carrying ammunition up the steep slopes overlooking the road. We had a good supply of captured Italian hand-grenades which were larger than the Soviet-made ones, with which we were more familiar, but which were nonetheless equally effective and, if anything, gave off a louder bang when they exploded: a useful additional asset in darkness.

Even as we scrambled to the heights above the road I heard a thundering noise to our rear and there, coming toward us with all speed, was a Fascist cavalry patrol. I ordered my volunteers to take up position among the boulders on the upper crests of the hill, as I reasoned that horses would not be able to operate freely in such broken ground, and we struggled into place and returned their fire. The mounted troops must have realized that we had wrested the advantage from them and that their horses were a liability on rock-strewn ground against determined infantry resistance, for they wheeled about and made off in search of an easier target against which to vent their anger and aggression. The dying rays of the sun flashed red on their sword blades as they made off, and I was left to think how incongruous mounted men appeared in the twentieth-century war we were fighting. Our hill-top position above the road which led to the River Ebro, along which our main force had withdrawn, with mountains behind and to the sides, provided a good deterrent to cavalry, but afforded us far less protection from the sporadic artillery fire that was directed at us as night fell. Even so, we sustained only a few very minor injuries and these were mainly caused by shell and boulder fragments which whistled through the air in the wake of each in-coming volley.

I was most anxious that the enemy should not attempt to storm our position during the night, so I gave orders that we should let go a few hand-grenades every so often. This probably had little effect but the grenades gave off a pleasing bang and a bright flash and I hoped that the Fascists down in the valley would be deceived into thinking that we had an anti-tank gun covering the pass and that this would cool their ardour to launch a sustained attack against our position – an attack which I knew could not be held for long and which would lead to the inevitable destruction of my small band. Occasionally we would supplement our grenade-throwing with a little rifle fire to suggest that we were fighting fit and a match for anything.

Around midnight I came to the conclusion that this make-believe had gone on quite long enough, and that we could really hope to achieve little more by maintaining our position as, with the coming of daylight, our true strength would be all too apparent to the Nationalists. I therefore gave the

word for us to pack up as much of our equipment as we could reasonably carry, to descend as quietly as possible back to the road, and set off with all speed to rejoin the larger force which by now had a six-hour start over us.

After a trouble-free night's march along the road we rejoined our comrades as they waited in the queue to cross the River Ebro over a bridge which linked Mora de Ebro to Mora la Nueva and carried the Zaragoza-Barcelona railway line. We must have been among the last Republican troops to use this route into Catalonia for we had not travelled far from the bridge when we heard Republican engineers firing the charges which sent it crashing down into the waters of the Ebro. The Fascist attempt to reach the sea at Tortosa was thus frustrated, and they concentrated their attack on Valencia, further south.

I imagine that Sam Wild must have included an account of my small part in the delaying action in his report to Brigade because a few days later the Commanding Officer of 35th Division, General 'Walter', Karol Swierczewski, officially confirmed my rank of lieutenant. Although I was glad of this news, what gave me more pleasure was that the day's defensive fighting near Gandesa had given the Listers time to take up position further down the River Ebro, and their efforts were to delay the Fascist advance for several more days so that the leading enemy forces did not reach the sea until 15th April, at Viñaroz. From then on, of course, Republican Spain was effectively divided into two and its problems were mounting rapidly.

With the River Ebro providing a clear defensive line we felt the tension of the last three weeks begin to fall away – only to be replaced by an overwhelming weariness. Some of the tension, however, could not be dispelled. Niggling away at the back of many minds was the question of whether the Nationalists would seek to push ahead across the Ebro and extend their victory. We were in no condition to offer much resistance should such a move have developed as, in common with so many of the Republican units which had retreated from Aragon, the British Battalion was in a very sorry state. It may simply have been my personal bias but I nevertheless thought at the time that we had perhaps managed to retain a greater sense of purpose and exhibited more resilience than was evidenced by other battalions in the XVth Brigade.

I had already witnessed the effect that the restoration of discipline could produce on the morale of even the most war-weary troops when Dunbar had rallied a collection of retreating soldiers outside Gandesa and given them an objective. I was now about to see it happen again. Ćopić, who had managed to escape from the fighting near Calaceite and

make his way across the Ebro into Catalonia, began to reorganize the XVth Brigade, to establish collecting points for the scattered battalions and for the stragglers who were still filtering in from Aragon, to gather supplies of food, clothes and weapons, and to provide medical treatment for the many who were suffering from wounds and sickness. Sam Wild was firmly back in the driving seat as Battalion Commander and Bob Cooney was appointed Political Commissar to replace Wally Tapsell. Wild and Cooney set about the task of restoring morale with a vengeance, for they fully realized that their men were far too preoccupied with the recent lengthy retreat. They appreciated that every one of us was aware of the immense Fascist superiority in men and weaponry, and also of the advantage which they held over us in terms of their organization and communications. Although there was no sense of defeatism in the air there was a lack of buoyancy and I know, from remarks that he made to me, that Sam feared that it would only take another successful Nationalist thrust to break our will to resist. He was determined that when the Fascist challenge next came we would be ready to meet it with all our old resolve. A series of meetings and discussions was held, at both brigade and battalion level, and the message was driven home of the need to resist, to fight and to fortify. Sam, perhaps more than anyone else I met in Spain, appreciated that men who were occupied, no matter how depressing the circumstances in which they found themselves, were far less likely to think of defeat than if they were left to their own devices. Hence working parties were established to dig defensive positions along the north bank of the Ebro and routine patrols became an integral part of our daily duties.

Visitors from Britain played their part in the rebuilding of morale. I remember in mid-April listening to an address given to the Battalion by Harry Pollitt who had flown out to Spain on learning of the losses we had sustained during the retreat. With his case containing cigarettes and letters from friends and relatives in Britain, Harry was a popular figure with the Battalion, but he also had a commanding presence, and he was a talented speaker. Although he cut a rather curious figure in the Spanish countryside in his blue three-piece suit and his collar and tie, his rousing speech was not lost on an audience who were impressed not only by its content but by the fact that it was delivered by a man who cared so much for our cause that he had undertaken the arduous journey from home to be with us. Harry later went on to spread the message of encouragement and hope to the sick and wounded in various hospitals throughout Catalonia and won himself more new friends and admirers as a result of his efforts. Nor was Harry the only one to visit the Battalion at that time.

Bill Forrest of *The News Chronicle* and Sefton Delmer of *The Daily Express* also came to talk to us, and the men responded warmly to them as they knew that here were two journalists who could be relied upon for their authentic reporting, in contrast to so much unfounded, ill-informed and partial rubbish which all too often passed for objective coverage of the war in the British press.

Gradually the old camaraderie and sense of purpose took a strong hold and received a further boost as the last big batch of volunteers from home joined us, along with a hard core of experienced fighters released by the closure of our training camps in the south and the slimming down of Brigade Staff. New equipment also reached us in considerable quantities from the Soviet Union following the French decision to reopen the frontier with Spain and its arrival added to the feeling that we had not been forgotten by the outside world.

Within a few days it became apparent that the Fascists had no immediate plans to force a crossing of the Ebro, and that they were fully occupied in launching their new offensive towards Valencia: their losses there were to be heavy as they met with strong resistance from Republican troops who were operating from carefully and strongly prepared defensive positions. Our patrols along the river bank were occasionally subjected to light rifle fire, but the front had settled down into a period of calm. The Battalion was pulled back to Mola for a spell of rest and training, something for which we felt a pressing need.

Finding enough food to feed the Battalion remained a problem even in the safety of Catalonia and scrounging and bartering became the order of the day. Our quest for food was urgent because of our poor physical shape at that time. For almost all of the previous month we had been engaged in a fighting retreat against vastly stronger forces, and you eat what you can when you can. Three meals a day was an enticing dream; one meal a day was a cherished hope. Frequently we went for days at a stretch with nothing whatsoever to eat. At one point in the retreat I can recollect some of my Spanish lads telling us of a particular tree the leaves of which, if chewed slowly and thoroughly, lessened the pangs of hunger. By that time we were all so starved that we were prepared to try almost anything to ease the pains which were constantly gnawing away inside our bellies. When we found one of these trees, we stripped it of all of its foliage. When we had finished only the topmost branches carried leaves, and the poor tree looked for all the world as if it had fallen victim to a plague of ravenous locusts. We munched away at the leaves, washing them down with a drop of liberated cognac, and the result was terrible. My stomach felt as if it had

been set on fire. True, the hunger pains had disappeared, but the discomfort which replaced them was every bit as bad as the original complaint! We had chronic indigestion for days afterwards, and I was never tempted to try that cure for hunger again.

During the lull, I spent a few days at the Divisional Machine-Gun School. There it was possible to buy a little local fruit but, except for this small luxury, the diet was a constant one of a small portion of dried fish, a few potatoes, a slice of bread and a plentiful supply of coffee. Meat and rice seemed to have disappeared both from the menu and from the face of the earth. Even the meagre helpings of dried fish had to be soaked overnight in water before they could be eaten and then the taste was dreadful. If the Duke of Wellington was correct in saying that an army marches on its stomach, then after April 1938, the Republican Army in Spain would never again have taken a single step. That it not only marched again but also fought again is a tribute to its leaders and its soldiers.

Our recovery period at Mola was short-lived, for in mid-May a new Republican offensive was launched on the Lerida sector across the River Segre, and our XVth Brigade moved to take up position some thirty miles behind the front. We in the British Battalion marched every step of the way – some fifty miles – and did so in pouring rain which never let up for a second. The first Republican attack made no impact and the Battalion moved back, this time to Marsa, without seeing any of the action. Best of all our return journey was made by truck!

Marsa was to be the setting for our Battalion's longest period of rest and training throughout the entire course of the war. Our camp was at the foot of a valley surrounded by steep-sided hills. Bushes on the valley bottom and on the slopes gave protection from the hot sun and welcome security from the prying gaze of the enemy's reconnaissance planes. The more ingenious and talented members of the Battalion constructed a number of brush huts in an amazing variety of architectural styles. There was rumoured to be a plan afoot to build an open-air theatre, but if this piece of grapevine news was true I cannot recall ever seeing any evidence of the finished product. If such extra-curricular activities provided an endless source of amusement, usually at the expense of their perpetrators, they were not allowed to detract from our prime purpose which was to prepare for the next engagement. A vigorous programme of military training and physical fitness was embarked upon as the Battalion again approached operational strength. These efforts were increased as midsummer drew nearer, for we all knew that it would not be long now before we were

required to re-enter the war. Reports were constantly reaching us of the fighting on the Valencian front, where our Republican forces, under General Miaja, were heroically resisting Fascist attacks and inflicting heavy casualties, and these left us in no doubt that we would soon be pressed into service to relieve the pressure on our comrades in the south. More visitors arrived to see us as the tempo of our training quickened, among them Pandit Nehru and Krishna Menon who, if I recall correctly, were accompanied from Barcelona to our base by two prominent members of the Republican Government, Alvarez del Vayo and Pablo de Azcarate.

By now the Battalion had a strength of 650 men of whom roughly a third were British. The new recruits who had joined us had been well-trained, certainly better trained than we had ourselves been in the early stages of the conflict, but for the first time Spanish conscripts, as opposed to Spanish volunteers, appeared in our ranks. A hard core of Anglo-Spanish veterans provided the Battalion with a disciplined focus around which the new troops coalesced, and rapidly the five companies came to form a coherent fighting unit. Nearly all of the British personnel in Spain who were fit for active service were now in the Battalion.

Although secrecy had never been a feature of life in the International Brigade, perhaps sometimes to the detriment of its efficiency, the changes which were introduced into the pattern of our training from the middle of June onward left us in no doubt as to what was to be our next objective. More and more emphasis was given to crossing a dry river-bed and then taking up positions to cover the crossing of others. Obviously the Republicans were going on the offensive, and intending to strike across the River Ebro. Once this dawned on us our morale rose and our confidence grew: the long retreat from Belchite became a thing of the past. Once again we were going to show our enemy and the world at large that the Republic was not prepared to meekly succumb to defeat. If the plan of campaign worked as intended, then the Catalonian forces would smash through the Fascist-held territory on the south bank of the River Ebro and eventually link up with Miaja's troops, who were still fighting very valiantly around Sagunto and Valencia. We knew that it would be our own efforts that would determine whether or not the plan would work and we were prepared to give of our all.

* * *

By April 1938 after twenty-one months of war the Republic was on the verge of collapse. As the Aragon Front dissolved the

military situation became desperate. The Republican Army was blasted out of its strongholds by fast-moving armoured columns and continually strafed from the air as it retreated hastily across the River Ebro into Catalonia. Compared to the stalemate at Brunete and Jarama the situation was extremely fluid. On 15th April the Nationalist Army reached the Mediterranean coast at Vinaroz, effectively dividing the Republic into two enclaves and adding further fuel to the boast that the war would be over within a matter of weeks. Behind the lines, the civilian population already enduring shortages of food, heating and transport was now faced with a further test, as Barcelona and Valencia came within striking distance of the Nationalist air force. Furthermore, supplies of munitions and food from the Soviet Union, which had been such a central factor in the Republican war effort, were dwindling rapidly. Although the Soviet Union pointed to the difficulty of maintaining supplies when its ships were exposed to submarine attack in the Mediterranean and alluded to the need to husband its own resources in the face of a growing threat from Japan in the Far East, it was evident that Stalin was beginning to lose faith in the ability of the Republic to continue to resist the Nationalist onslaught.

Yet, despite the odds stacked against it, the Republic was to fight on for a further twelve months. In many ways, the fact that it was able to sustain the war effort into 1939 was a tribute to the resilience and determination of those who fought under the Republican banner although arguably they were assisted by two strokes of good fortune in the spring of 1938. Certainly Franco's decision to strike south towards the Republican capital of Valencia instead of pursuing the retreating Republican Army across the Ebro was a tactical error. By turning away from Catalonia the Nationalists forsook the opportunity to crush the industrial heartland of the Republic and eliminate its last surviving land frontier with France. In addition, Franco committed his forces to a campaign in difficult terrain where his tank formations were of limited value in dislodging the stubborn rearguard actions staged by the Republican Army. The decision to move against Valencia rather than Catalonia, therefore, gave the Republic a vital breathing space but even this would probably only have been a temporary respite if it had not been accompanied by the reappointment of Léon Blum as Premier of France in March 1938. Blum, a

Socialist, who had headed the first Popular Front administration in France, responded to Negrín's pleas and reopened the previously sealed Franco-Spanish frontier. In the following months food and war material poured over the border into Catalonia. In addition the Soviet Union which could now funnel its supplies through French ports stepped up the flow of weapons to the Republican Army.

By July 1938 the Republican Army in Catalonia had been given three vital months to regroup behind the natural defensive position provided by the fast-flowing River Ebro. Furthermore, it had been brought up to strength with new conscripts and re- equipped with an assorted array of weaponry imported from France or hastily manufactured in the factories of Barcelona. It was time to once

Spain July 1938

again take the offensive for despite the difficulties encountered by the Nationalist forces in their campaign against Valencia, they were now within twenty miles of the city. It was anticipated that a major assault across the Ebro would initially divert attention away from Valencia and ultimately provide a springboard for a campaign to re-unite the two Republican zones. The attack was entrusted to Colonel Jose Modesto who by the evening of 24th July 1938 had massed 100,000 men plus what field guns and aircraft the Republican Army still had at its disposal. The aim was to cross the Ebro on a twenty-mile front at a point where it was lightly defended and to push quickly through the enemy lines. The fact that the army would cross at night and proceed over largely inhospitable terrain suggested quite clearly that Modesto was aware of the need to minimize the role that could be played by the Nationalist air force and tank formations in the initial assault.

6

The Battle of the River Ebro

In the night of 23rd/24th July, we in the XVth Brigade began to take up our positions close to the River Ebro, where other units of the Republican forces were also assembling. When it was still dark, the crossing began, and what a contrast it was to our retreat into Catalonia from Aragon that spring. Everywhere detailed organization and military precision were evident. Unlike the dispirited troops who had then trekked forlornly into Catalonia in chaos and disorder, we were filled with confidence. Some may be sceptical that such a transformation could have been brought about, that a retreating, disorganized force could have been rebuilt, in so short a time, into one in which victory was considered not simply as a possibility but as a certainty. As we prepared to cross the Ebro again, I did not meet a single individual who entertained the thought of defeat. Surely no army has ever been blessed with troops more resilient, determined and resolute than those who fought in the ranks of the Republican forces in the Spanish Civil War, and this fact, perhaps more than any other, has always made the Nationalists' victory a bitter pill to swallow. Without the massive military support that the Fascists received from Germany and Italy, I am sure that the outcome of the war would have been totally different. Even to this day, and try as I might, I simply cannot believe that the efforts of the indigenous Fascists in Spain could conceivably have defeated the defenders of the Republic. I cannot believe it. I will not believe it.

We crossed the mighty River Ebro in boats, each rowed by two local Spanish civilians whose knowledge of the river's currents and landing places was indispensable. The small size of the boats meant that they could carry only six troops at a time and such was the weight of men and equipment that their gunwales were perilously close to the surface of the water. Any sudden movement by the occupants and water slopped over the sides and swilled about inside. So strong were the currents and so heavily laden the boats that we crossed the river at an angle rather than steering a straight course between the two banks.

The Mac Paps were the first unit of the XVth Brigade to complete the crossing, near Asco, and overcame initial resistance by the Fascists so that the British Battalion was untroubled by enemy machine-gun and rifle fire, but shells were falling around us as we huddled low inside the boats. Fortunately, the Nationalists' artillery was firing blind, and although exploding shells sent uncomfortably large waves to toss our small craft vigorously up and down and from side to side, casualties were minimal. Just as well, because the Ebro was broad and deep and the heavily encumbered occupants of any boat struck by shell or pierced by shrapnel would have had little chance of swimming to safety, even if they had been lucky enough to survive the first impact.

It was a marvellous moment when we climbed out of the boats and scrambled up the south bank. What exhilaration! We were on the move again, we were taking the initiative and we were on top of the world. Our instructions were to move westward, inland, by-passing any opposition, toward Corbera and Gandesa, and then to sever the main road used by the enemy between Aragon and the front. We moved in open order away from the river and along the road to Corbera. Only occasionally were we troubled by rifle and machine-gun fire from Nationalist units which had been left behind to delay us or which had been cut off by our advance. This area lay south of the Venta de Camposina – Pueblo de Corbera road, and as we swept up the low hills to flush out the Moorish troops, one of my Company shouted out, 'George is hit'. George Stockdale was officially the company clerk, but he was many other things as well: company quartermaster, postman and messenger. He even served as our first-aid man; this arose because whenever the Battalion was at rest behind the lines our doctor would call for volunteers from each Company to undertake a little training in first aid. I 'volunteered' George. After a few hours' training he returned as the proud owner of a bag of bandages and boasting that he could deal with every complaint except a pregnancy. George had joined the newly formed company which I had trained at Tarazona de la Mancha in the autumn of 1937 and for some inexplicable reason I had designated him as the company clerk. He had grumbled at my decision and argued that he had come to Spain to be a soldier and that he could have stayed at home and been a clerk, but I eventually managed to persuade him to accept the job. George had a thick Yorkshire accent and, like everybody else, he tried to learn a few words of Spanish, but his accent and Spanish seemed totally incompatible. The Spanish lads in the Battalion were always very helpful to anyone trying to speak their language, but George's efforts were inevitably met with bemused smiles.

George had come north from Tarazona with a group sent to reinforce the Battalion after its losses at Teruel and he was allowed to stay with me and continue as company clerk. Together we had taken part in the retreat from Aragon and in the long defence at the Ebro. When I heard that George had been wounded, I rushed to him and found him lying among the sweet-smelling herbs which grow in Aragon. He was in a very bad way. A bullet from a concealed machine-gun nest had struck him in the head, just above the left eye, and had cut a dreadful groove in his skull from front to back leaving his brain exposed. George tried to speak and I knelt to listen. I put my ear to his mouth but all I heard was the sound of death as his last breath rattled in his throat. I thought of his wife back home in Leeds of whom he had spoken so often and so tenderly, and for a moment

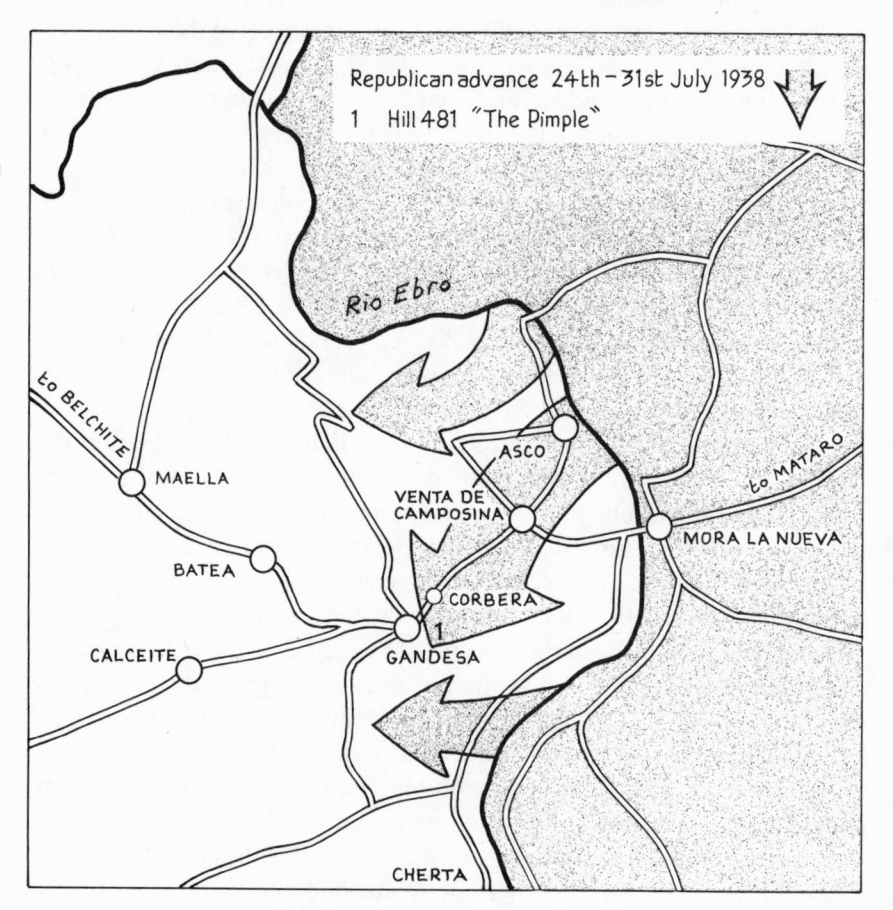

The Crossing of the Ebro July 1938

Right: Moorish troops fighting on the Nationalist side

Below: Machine-gunners of the British Battalion digging in at Brunete

Left: A ruined church in Belchite left by Franco as a permanent war memorial

Right: A street in Belchite where bitter hand-to-hand fighting took place

Below: Nationalist prisoners being led away after the capture of Purburell Hill

I wished that she could be beside him; but it was too late. If I could have wept for anyone in Spain, it would have been for George. We had been through so much together since our first meeting and now he was the first of my Company to die in the Ebro crossing.

With the coming of dawn, the Fascist air force detected us and their bombers which had been flown north from the Levante front began strafing us. By mid-afternoon we were only a few miles from Corbera and things were looking good. The XIIIth Brigade had been detailed to take Corbera, but found its flank threatened by a force of Moorish troops dug-in on the steep-sided hills. We in the British Battalion were, therefore, ordered to lend support to them to help to clear the area. It was late in the afternoon before this operation was fully underway and it proved difficult to drive the battle-hardened Moors from their prepared positions, especially as they were well-versed in mountain warfare. But after several hours of confused fighting the hills belonged to us.

Earlier that evening I had another close brush with death. We had just occupied the top of a hill, by the simple expedient of charging up its slopes and firing furiously as we went, and as my troops settled themselves down in some shrubs just below the crest and prepared to repel any invaders, I decided to take a look to see where the nearest enemy position was situated. From the hill which we had seized the land fell away only to rise quite sharply again into another pinnacle. I felt unsure as to whether or not the retreating Fascists would have chosen to make a stand there and felt that this was something which should be investigated before darkness fell. It was sunset as I began to crawl toward the dip in the ground which divided the two hills and the full rays of the sun were shining straight into my face making it difficult for me to see anything. As I left the protective covering of a clump of bushes, all around me clods of earth leapt into the air, as bullets were sprayed by a Fascist marksman who had been lying in wait for some idiot to come that way, knowing full well that the high land he held and the light from the setting sun behind him gave him an overwhelming advantage. Sure enough an idiot had materialized! If my opponent's aim had matched his strategic skills I would have been a 'goner'. As it was I managed to wriggle hastily back into the cover of the bushes and complete my retreat under the covering fire of my own troops. My stupidity appalled me. There I was, a fully fledged lieutenant, a veteran fighter in Spain, once again acting like the rawest of raw recruits.

We had now been on the move for twenty-four hours, continually advancing over open country and in combat, and the strain was beginning to show. A captured Fascist position had yielded an ample supply of food,

but we were badly in need of rest. This luxury we were to be denied, for, next day, the Nationalist High Command reacted to our audacious attack which had threatened its avenue to the sea.

The Fascists called into action aircraft, artillery and troops drawn from other fronts. This meant that the river crossings and our newly-gained footholds in Aragon were subjected to a constant bombardment. More troubling was the disruption of the movement of our rather limited reserves to the front. However, this did not delay the advance of the British Battalion, which was now charged with eradicating Fascist resistance on a hillside designated 'Hill 481', and which will always be remembered by those who survived the fighting on its inhospitable slopes as the 'Pimple'. Strategically, that landmark was the key to Gandesa. If we could take it, then Gandesa was ours for the asking. It lay about a mile to the east of the town and was almost within sight of the pass where Malcolm Dunbar had rallied our retreating forces to stem the Fascist advance and cover the withdrawal into Catalonia. The 'Pimple' itself was a rocky hill which rose sharply, so that its uppermost reaches were almost like a precipice. The Fascists had not wasted a moment when this important feature had been in their possession, for it had been strongly fortified with concrete bunkers, trenches and barbed wire. When I first saw this formidable obstacle I had the strange feeling that I had seen it before, perhaps from the nearby pass. I reasoned that this was impossible as the undulating ground between the pass and the 'Pimple' would have obscured the hilly outcrop from my view. Gradually light dawned. My God! Did it not look all too similar to Purburell Hill? Would we have to pay a similar high price for the 'Pimple' to that which we had paid for Purburell Hill? Heaven forbid! To do the seemingly impossible once is one thing, to do it twice is beyond the bounds of credibility. Yet the 'Pimple' had to be taken and it had fallen to us to take it.

We launched our first assault against the 'Pimple' on 27th July. Only then did we come to appreciate fully the strength of the position which our enemy held. Many of his machine-guns were sited in places virtually invulnerable to attack, and we had to advance over open ground with but the minimum of cover to protect our assaults. Height, cover and preparation all worked to the advantage of the Fascist defenders. Our first attempt was repelled with heavy casualties as were those which were launched over the next six days, but I was not destined to see all of those attacks. As though the enemy defences on the 'Pimple' were not sufficient in themselves to wreak havoc among our attacking units, we found that we were also being subjected to fire on our flank from Fascist positions on the

surrounding heights. To add to our misery even the church and larger buildings in Gandesa itself gave safe cover to the opposing machine-gunners from which to direct a torrent of lead against us. It seemed at times that every hand was set against us, especially when enemy artillery, which had been rushed to the front in great number, joined in pouring an almost continuous fire into our positions. And how lamentably weak were our positions! The ground was unyielding and only where there was a light covering of soil was it possible to dig trenches, and these were so shallow that it was only by lying flat in them that any protection could be gained from the enemy's guns. Everywhere were rocks which cracked and disintegrated with the force of incoming bullets and high explosive shells. Yet this miserable few acres of land was 'our patch' and the pitifully inadequate and uncomfortably shallow trenches were our 'homes' in which we lived, fought and died. There was no cover to shield us from the scorching rays of the sun which blazed down upon us, and excrement, blood, the sweat on our bodies and the few scraps of food which had fallen to the earth brought legions of flies to torment us. All supplies, ammunition, food and water had to be manhandled over the rocks to the front line under cover of darkness. We were all exhausted and weak from the heat, inadequate food, the chronic shortage of liquid and the total absence of sleep. The plight of the severely wounded was especially pitiful. Many had to endure hours of agony under the heat of a remorseless sun before the safety of night descended and they could receive something more than the most superficial medical treatment. Even then they had to face up to the daunting prospect of being dragged and heaved across the broken ground to the rear positions which only added to the pain they were already experiencing.

On 30th July, it fell to my Company, No. 2 Company, to lead another assault on the 'Pimple'. Just before dawn we started our cautious ascent, crawling from rock to rock, keeping as low as possible, and trying to leave the loose shale undisturbed, lest the sound of cascading rock fragments alert the enemy to our presence. We had moved but a short distance beyond our own front line when we were greeted by a fusillade of rifle and machine-gun fire and any semblance of an orderly advance disappeared as each man sought cover for himself. John Angus, who was acting as the Company Commander and was a lieutenant like myself, was wounded and, as the senior officer, I took command. There was nothing that I could do to regain the momentum of our attack, as we were now pinned down by continuous enemy fire; it was now simply a matter of returning fire whenever each man thought that it was safe enough for him to expose

himself for as long as it took to discharge a few rounds of ammunition at the heights above. If we could not move forward without inviting instant death then nor could we retreat without presenting an inviting target. All we could do was stay put and wait for nightfall. What a prospect! Twelve hours of lying on rocky soil, every fragment of which seemed intent on burying itself in our bodies, of being continually shot at, of having nothing to eat or drink, of being driven half-mad by the ceaseless attention of the most malevolent flies in the whole of Spain, and of hoping that by staying still the attention of a Fascist marksman would be distracted by movement elsewhere.

Around midday, while trying to ascertain the exact positions of my scattered command, I must have presented a little too much of my body to the enemy, for I felt a blow in my neck which hurled me round and threw me flat on my back. Clearly, I had given away my location by bobbing about to espy my comrades, and a sharp-shooter had spotted me and bided his time until I gave him a clear target. I have to credit my assailant with superb shooting. He fired just once and he hit me. Beautiful shooting; but luckily for me not quite good enough. Two of the lads nearest to me crawled stealthily alongside to take a look at my wound. I was not in much pain, just bleeding copiously from where the bullet had passed right through the fleshy part of my neck. More disturbing than the flow of blood was the fact that I could not move my head. They bandaged me up as best as they could but clearly I could no longer carry on in a position of command, so I handed over leadership of the Company to Sergeant Bill Harrington who did a sterling job until he too was wounded. Corporal Joe Harkins then stepped into the breach and carried on the good work until he was killed. Many times throughout that wretched day I thought that the sun was never going to set. When darkness finally came the other wounded and myself were evacuated from the 'Pimple'. Because of the chaos the enemy had caused to our supply lines, medical treatment was not close at hand. Those who could walk began to make their way back toward the River Ebro; others, who were too badly wounded to fend for themselves, were carried either on stretchers or on the backs of their comrades. If the long haul back to the Ebro was punishing on the wounded, it must also have been purgatory for the weakened men who bore them.

A pontoon bridge had been constructed at a narrow point of the river but, because of constant enemy air and artillery attack, had not been strengthened sufficiently to take heavy vehicles. Towards the end of the day as I drew closer to the Ebro I could see one of the many air-raids on

the pontoons. The ground shook under the impact of the falling bombs and great clouds of water and débris were flung into the air. I reached the bank of the river only to see that the bridge I wanted to use had been damaged. However, as I could also hear the roar of the next wave of approaching bombers and having no idea as to whether they were about to continue their attack on 'my bridge' or if they were intent on some other target, I decided to cross. The moorings of the boats used to make the pontoon bridge had been loosened by the repeated bombardments and many of the wooden planks which linked them had either been destroyed or displaced. Frequently, I had to swim from boat to boat and balance over the turbulent waters on one wobbling plank, but I finally managed to set foot on the far bank and, apart from being rather short of breath, I was unscathed. On the north bank of the river a fleet of lorries ferried the wounded to the railway-siding at Pradell-Torre de Fontabella, and from there trains crawled across Catalonia to Barcelona, where the seriously injured were disembarked, and then on northwards to Mataro where hospital beds awaited those of us with more superficial damage.

The hospital at Mataro was small, having been a minor convent in the days of peace, and I was put to bed in a minute room. The occupant of the adjoining bed was a man who was later to make a name for himself back home as a great trades union leader and more recently he has earned acclaim as a formidable campaigner for old-age pensioners: Jack Jones. Jack had been laid low by a wound in his shoulder which did not respond readily to treatment and eventually he was sent back to England. It did not require great perception to see how desperate was the plight of Republican Spain: a simple and cursory glance around the hospital at Mataro revealed all. Food was in short supply; what little there was never changed. The local civilians had no surplus to sell to the hospital. This was in complete contrast to my previous experience in hospitals in Murcia and Madrid.

A qualified doctor was, however, on hand. He took a good look at my neck and told a nurse to dress it with fresh bandages to replace those which had been fixed on the battlefield. Although there was material for sewing up wounds, there was not enough available except for in extremely bad cases. Clearly the injury to my neck did not fall into that category, and as my earlier wounds had healed without infection developing I saw no reason why I should receive medical supplies needed far more urgently by others. The wound was painful but that was to be expected and I knew that it would simply be a matter of time before it healed and mobility returned.

I had only been at Mataro for a few days when Sam Wild appeared along with two or three other comrades from the Battalion. They had come to the hospital with a sackful of mail for the wounded and Sam asked how I was feeling. Having seen the plight of so many of my fellow fighters I felt it honest to reply that I was well on the way to recovery.

'You don't look right yet,' said Sam, 'but we're off the "Pimple". We couldn't take it and now we're in a reserve position. There's a lot to be done and we can use you. How about coming back with us? There's a lorry outside and you can travel in the back. We'll just have to make sure that no one sees you trying to leave 'cos if they do you'll be back in that bed in no time.'

How could I turn down such an offer? Sam grabbed my freshly laundered uniform, threw an arm round me to lend me some support, and had me out of the hospital and into the back of the waiting lorry in a matter of minutes. He threw a few old sacks over me and said that he would help me to get dressed later when there was time. The journey back to the Battalion was not one I would care to repeat.

Sam, as always, had been quite fair with me. He had not forced me to leave Mataro and the Battalion was in a reserve position, but still under sporadic enemy artillery fire and with a Republican battery firing over our heads. Like innumerable others before me I went back to war swathed in bandages. To be honest, things were so desperate by that time that anyone who could hold a gun was considered, and considered themselves, to be ready for front-line duty. If anything I was in better shape than many in the Battalion's ranks for my neck wound had knitted together and was free of infection, so there really was nothing to prevent me from taking charge of my Company.

By now our offensive had been well and truly halted. Enemy planes brought north in great numbers from the Levante front kept up continuous bombing sorties against our rear especially those roads leading to the river crossings. Nevertheless, there was an opportunity for the weary troops to catch up on some much needed sleep. Parcels containing chocolate and tobacco had arrived from Britain and were distributed among the men, and life took on a semblance of normality. I enjoyed three days of this decadence before orders were received for the Battalion to ready itself for more front-line service.

The front line was now the Sierra Pandols where a huge concentration of Fascist forces – some 100,000 men with massive artillery support – had been assembled in readiness to seize the heights which dominated Mora de Ebro and the river crossings. Our entire front was endangered, as it

seemed that only the Listers stood in the enemy's way, and they had been so weakened by constant attacks that they could have no hope of beating off a new challenge of such magnitude. It fell to us to relieve the Listers and we began an exhausting march across open country. We knew what we were in for and there was little joy in our ranks; but we also knew how significant the forthcoming action was to be. We passed through the bomb- and shell-shattered ruins of Pinell and Prat de Campte on our route to the Sierra Pandols, and looked forlornly at the rocky, bare earth which surrounded us and which would surely defy our entrenching tools.

When the massive Fascist war machine was hurled into action the British Battalion was more fortunate than other battalions of the XVth Brigade for it escaped the full force of the enemy's initial offensive. We were troubled by artillery fire which claimed a steadily mounting number of casualties but we were not so hard pressed ourselves that we could not send out companies in support of the Lincolns and the Mac Paps who were receiving a heavy mauling. We did, however, launch a successful concerted attack against an outlying spur of Hill 666 which was the key to the entire Pandols sector.

On 24th August it was our turn to feel the full weight of the Fascist advance. We had barely taken over the Lincolns' position on the main heights of the Pandols when the enemy launched its biggest and most sustained attack yet on this sector of the front. An artillery barrage, the like of which none of us had ever experienced, crashed down around us and flying shrapnel and rock splinters inflicted dozens of minor injuries. As soon as the barrage lifted, two Fascist infantry battalions hurled themselves against us. Although still reeling from the shock waves of the barrage we stood our ground and repelled the Fascists but only after bitter fighting in which the Battalion received heavy casualties. That night we were relieved by a Spanish unit, and later we received a citation from the Brigade and the 35th Division for our efforts in holding Hill 666 against such incredibly superior odds.

A few days' rest followed, but again our enjoyment was marred by periodic artillery fire. It seemed that now we were in the front line for shorter periods before being given a break of a few days, but that when we were at the sharp end things were infinitely worse than they had been earlier in the war. Clearly, the Fascists' strength had not ebbed but was increasing in a steady progression until it had now reached such a size that it threatened to engulf us whenever we opposed it. Still, we had not broken even under the tremendous pounding we had taken at Hill 666. Nationalist incursions into the front we had re-established in Aragon had

been restricted to a depth of only two, or at most three, miles; and this had been achieved after forty-three days of vicious and continuous fighting. They may have had more men, more planes, more artillery, more everything, but we were not yet ready to believe them to be invincible. Even so we could not help but ask, 'How much more have they got? How much more can we take?' We were to find partial answers to both of these questions a few days later when the Fascists launched their greatest offensive of the war in the Sierra Caballs.

Two hundred enemy guns opened up on a one-mile front and were supported by almost continuous flights of bombers. When subjected to this weight of attack with no large calibre guns or planes to match it, it is not surprising that the Republican front wavered and then broke. The entire XVth Brigade was rushed by truck along roads made perilous by a steady bombardment to plug the gaps which had appeared. We barely had time to disembark from our vehicles and rub the soreness and stiffness from our aching limbs before being sent into action at Sandesco where we managed quickly to drive the Fascist infantry from a position they had recently taken.

It was said at the time that during the fighting in the Sierras the Fascist air force was dropping 10,000 bombs a day. I do not know how accurate this was but I am quite prepared to believe it. After the brief skirmish at Sandesco, and when the front had temporarily stabilized, the sector which my Company was told to patrol contained a ravine in which an armoured car had been stationed. The Nationalist observers must have noted our whereabouts for, early one otherwise trouble-free afternoon we all saw an enemy squadron curving round in the sky to our left. We knew instinctively who was going to provide a target for the enemy bombers – us! As the planes straightened to begin their approach to our positions we could see the dark shapes of bombs falling from beneath them. We had no trenches, no protection, we just lay flat on the ground with our arms covering our heads. The bombs burst all about us. The impact was terrific. The ground trembled and heaved, and clouds of swirling dust reduced visibility to a few inches. Some perhaps prayed for a safe deliverance from the holocaust which engulfed us; I cursed the Fascists and the Non Intervention Committee, and those back home who were too blind to see what was happening in Spain, with every blasphemy I could summon to my trembling lips. I do not think I recovered from that bombing for a very long time. Had I been in the British forces I am sure that I could not only have legitimately gone sick with 'shock', but that I would have been made to do so; there were neither the facilities nor the encouragement for such a course of action in Spain.

If the bombing was horrendous, the constant barrages of artillery fire which we attracted right from the outset of our offensive across the Ebro were little better, and probably the cumulative effect of them was every bit as detrimental as the more sporadic heavy bombing. Obviously not all of the artillery shells exploded, and I can remember seeing several duds lying on the ground in almost pristine condition. I was amazed at their size. They must have been three feet long with a diameter little short of twelve inches. Once anyone had seen one of those duds they had an altogether different attitude to future artillery barrages! Frequently the flash of the heavy guns could be seen as the deadly missiles were fired, and then, as though at once, the sound of the discharge, the howl of the approaching shell and the impact as it hit its target. How we came to hate planes and cannon and how different would have been our sentiments if they had been ours and not those of the Fascists; but they never were.

Once the front had stabilized the Battalion was withdrawn from this sector and placed in reserve on the Asco-Corbera road. Even in the rest areas conditions had deteriorated quite remarkably, for the débris of battle seemed to lie everywhere. The Ebro valley that had once looked so very beautiful, a swath of green between infertile, barren hills, now lay denuded. Nut trees and grape vines had been smashed and destroyed to become but a part of the larger desolation that inevitably accompanies war. We continued to have casualties from artillery fire and aerial bombing for rest areas were no longer safe areas, just patches of relative calm in a landscape of noise, chaos, danger and death. Nor was the price of war evident only in the fields and on the hills. Of the 150 men of my Company who had crossed the Ebro on the night of 25th July, I had just under two dozen still with me. The rest were either dead, wounded or missing. I fear that many more were lying under the shallow, gravelly soil of the Sierras than were regaining their strength between the clean sheets of hospital beds. No longer was it possible to think in terms of sergeants and corporals, for now just a small band of exhausted and emaciated troops clustered around me as their leader. If I was scared stiff I had to keep it to myself and still offer them leadership, without which all semblance of order and military discipline would have disappeared. Every single one of those lads was a hero to me and no matter how weary, forlorn, desperate and afraid I felt I was determined that I would do my best by them. I owed them so very much and they expected so very little in return.

On 18th September yet another Fascist push was made against the entire Caballs-Pandols sector. The British Battalion was called to the front and its weary troops disturbed from their sleep in the middle of the night to meet

this new threat. For once our front held, and we were all able to return somewhat belatedly to our slumbers. Again our respite was to be brief, and we were recalled to the front on 23rd September. Sam Wild had been wounded in our last action and had been forced to go to hospital for treatment, despite his loud and prolonged protestations. As before, George Fletcher assumed command in Sam's place. Our numbers had been supplemented by the addition of some 130 Spanish lads into our ranks but they were raw recruits, novices to the savagery of war, and my heart went out to them as they took in the scenes of devastation through frightened eyes. Now it has been said more than once that even before we boarded the trucks which would take us to the front we knew that this was to be our last action. It has been contended that we were aware that Prime Minister Negrín had expressed the intention of disbanding the International Brigades on 24th September in an effort to gain international support for the withdrawal of all foreign troops from Spain. While some members of the British Battalion and some members of the XVth Brigade may have known of Negrín's intentions, I most certainly did not. Nor for that matter do I know of one man in my Company who knew what was afoot. As far as No 2 Company was concerned we were simply going into action again: we had no inkling that we were about to embark on our final fight with the Fascists. Even had we done so I do not think that it would have made the slightest difference to us. We had been through so much that one more attack had no particular significance. The numbing and debilitating effects of war and exhaustion had made us almost blasé about danger; perhaps a few had even begun to see death as a release, but they would have been a small minority.

We were ferried toward the front with all speed in a convoy of lorries, frequently subjected to heavy artillery fire. Initially we were positioned to the rear of a threatened sector. Ahead of us, in the Sierra del Lavall de la Torre, the XIIIth International Brigade, Dombrowski, had taken terrible punishment. Only a few men from each of its units were still able to offer resistance when we moved into the sector of the front south of the Corbera-Venta de Camposina road. To put it bluntly our sector was in one hell of a mess. All of our positions were dominated by the higher ground which lay in Fascist hands. To our left were the Mac Paps. To our right, and on the far side of the road, were the Lincolns. Running along beside the road was a small stream which was flanked on each side by a dense mass of canes. We began to dig trenches in the thin, stony soil but, as always our trenches afforded protection only to crouching men.

My Company's position was forward of our main force. To ensure that I could readily see any threats which emerged and respond to them quickly, I placed myself in the middle of the trench. I despatched a few of my men, mixed Spanish and British, under the command of Frank West, to my right so that our right flank terminated close to the stream and road. To the left a trench which had been dug earlier by the Dombrowski's climbed part way up a hill toward the positions occupied by the Mac-Paps. This trench, which was the deepest part of our defensive line, had a partially completed gun position which we made haste to finish. There I stationed George Green with a Soviet-made machine-gun, a Dektorov. George had gained a fluency in Spanish during his lengthy service with the Battalion and I had no hesitation in providing him with an exclusively Spanish gun crew.

With the coming of first light I realized just how precarious was our position. If the enemy were to turn his guns upon us it would have been impossible for us to bring up supplies of men, ammunition, food and drink. Nor would we have any way of evacuating the wounded. The enemy front-line trench was desperately close to our own: so close in fact that I am sure that had we had anyone with the throwing arm of a good amateur cricketer it would have been possible to hurl a grenade across the narrow no-man's-land which separated us. Our parlous plight did not long escape the eyes of the Fascists and early on the morning of 23rd September their artillery opened up with a terrific barrage. My own Company, being so close to the Fascists' front-line trenches, escaped unscathed from this terrible fire, for had their gunners aimed directly at us they would have run the risk of blasting their own troops to smithereens. Battalion headquarters, which lay some way to the rear of our position, took a horrendous hammering, and counted something in the order of one shell every second landing on the Battalion's sector of the front, to say nothing of the carnage occasioned by the presence of over 200 planes which bombed and strafed our forces at will.

For hour after hour we lay pressed to the earth as this storm of death and destruction played over us. Every so often I would steel myself to peer over the low parapet of the trench toward the Fascists' front line to see if I could discern any signs of their infantry preparing to advance against us. To my left, I could see George Green doing exactly the same. I suppose it must have been approaching midday before the barrage was lifted and the enemy felt confident enough to advance against us. Even then, five tanks were sent in ahead of the infantry just in case the barrage, bombing and strafing had not done all that was expected of them. With help from our

Machine-Gun Company to the rear, we knocked out three of the tanks, and exacted a heavy toll from the troops who had moved forward *en masse* behind the protection of their armoured hulls. The two remaining tanks went on beyond our position. Suddenly I heard shouting away to my right and then I saw that the lads I had positioned there were standing with their hands raised in submission. I remembered thinking 'What the hell is going on here? I'm in command so why are those idiots acting so bloody stupidly?' The answer was all too obvious when I saw that enemy troops had managed to work their way round behind my right flank, probably by using the cane-covered sides of the stream to conceal their approach. On looking behind me I saw more Fascist troops advancing on my part of the trench. I shouted a warning to George on my left but before he and his crew had time to realign their machine-gun we were completely surrounded. There was nothing else for it but to accept the inevitability of my capture. At this juncture a little bit of quick thinking probably saved my life because I took the precaution of hastily removing my jacket and of pulling the loose, dusty parapet of the trench over it to obscure it from a casual glance, since in one of its pockets was a pass entitling Teniente Gregory to visit all parts of the Eastern Front. I did not want to be taken into captivity with that document on me for I was certain that its presence would have earned me a short, quick march to the nearest wall and the position of honour at a firing-squad.

Surrounded by enemy troops we were pushed toward the opposing front line. I kept looking behind me in the hope of seeing George and his crew, but they never came. I doubt if they ever left the trench, since the Fascists had made it a policy to shoot machine-gunners on the spot. After reaching the safety of the enemy's rear lines the dozen or so of us who had been taken prisoner were split up and I was left to stand alone outside a tent with only a hostile-looking guard for company. After some time he asked me if I had eaten and when I told him that I had not, he invited me to enter the tent which housed a long trestle table covered with places holding the remains of what had obviously been the midday meal of stew. I lost no time in piling all of the cold, greasy remnants of what had earlier been a more than passable lunch on to one plate and then I set about eating it. I had not had anything approaching a decent meal in the month since I had left hospital and I just picked up the food with my fingers and shoved it into my mouth. The guard simply stood there looking at me and then he started to laugh. Clearly the spectacle of me making a pig of myself was one which he thought should be shared and he called some of his comrades into the tent to join in the mirth. I did not give a damn! That

cold stew seemed like the perfect meal to me, and I am sure that I would have enjoyed it even more had I known that it was to be the one and only act of kindness I was to receive from my Fascist gaolers.

* * *

What had opened as a rapier thrust across the River Ebro eventually developed into one of the most bloody and protracted confrontations of the war. Over a period of almost four months the two armies stood toe to toe along a twenty-five-mile front engaged in a furious battle which claimed over 100,000 casualties. The appointment of General Garcia Volino, known to his troops as 'The Gravedigger', to command the Nationalist forces in September 1938 indicated that Franco would not be content merely to contain the Republican advance but intended to mount a massive counter-offensive designed to annihilate the Republican forces in Catalonia almost irrespective of the cost.

After the fast-flowing opening phases of the battle the engagement was transformed into trench warfare, as the Nationalist infantry, supported by massive artillery barrages, sought to dislodge the Republican forces now cast in a defensive role, grimly hanging on to the territory so recently wrested from the enemy. Despite the initial success of the Republican Army in holding the Nationalist counter-offensive Negrín appreciated that his forces were now engaged in a war of attrition in which the enemy had access to both superior numbers and equipment. With Franco contemptuously dismissing any suggestion of a negotiated settlement, other than on the basis of unconditional capitulation by the Republic, Negrín realized that his Government could only be saved by international intervention. In a dramatic speech delivered in September 1938 at Geneva to the League of Nations the Republican Premier offered to withdraw the International Brigades from Spain under the supervision of observers appointed by the League. In fact the Brigades had suffered horrifying casualties during the first six weeks of the Ebro campaign after repeatedly being used as a spearhead force. Even before the battle had opened, foreign volunteers only provided approximately one in four of the fighting-strength of many battalions and after almost two months of front-line activity the number of volunteers within the Republican Army was probably as little as 12,000. Therefore,

at little real cost to the Republican war effort, Negrín sought to curry favour with Britain and France, and also proportionately increase the pressure on Italy and Germany to withdraw their assistance to Franco. His hopes, however, were effectively dashed on 29th September 1938 when Britain and France surrendered to Hitler's demands for the annexation of the Sudetenland from Czechoslovakia. If Britain and France had chosen to fight to save Czechoslovakia, the Republic might have been saved, as it could have allied itself to an international anti-Fascist front. The Anglo-French capitulation clearly indicated that Negrín could expect little positive assistance from the western democracies. Perhaps more significantly the Munich Agreement destroyed Stalin's remaining faith in the effectiveness of collective security. After October 1938 the Soviet Union began to explore the possibility of improving relations with Germany as a means of deflecting the growing menace posed by Hitler's ambitions in eastern Europe. In this context the Spanish imbroglio was seen by Moscow as both a drain on Soviet military resources and as a factor which inhibited the development of an understanding with Nazi Germany. It was apparent, therefore, that by the turn of 1938 the Soviet Union, while continuing to render token support to the Republic, had effectively abandoned the Republican cause and indeed was coming to the conclusion that its interests would be best served by an end to the war.

Stalin's decision to woo Germany was probably the final nail in the Republic's coffin. Partly as a result of Soviet pressure and largely because he still clung to the hope of eliciting support for the withdrawal of all foreign 'volunteers' from Spain, Negrín elected to proceed with the evacuation of the International Brigades towards the end of 1938. The British Battalion fought its last, and ironically one of its most costly, engagements on the Ebro front on 23rd September 1938. After an emotional farewell parade through Barcelona on 15th November 1938, where they were addressed by Negrín and Dolores Ibarruri, 'La Pasionaria', the Battalion was transported through northern Catalonia and into France. The 300 survivors received a tumultuous welcome when they arrived at Victoria Station on 7th December 1938 to be dismissed for the last time by their acting commander Sam Wild.

Yet while the men of the British Battalion listened to the plaudits heaped upon them by Clement Attlee, Stafford Cripps and Willie

Gallacher they were aware that many of their comrades had been left behind in Nationalist prison camps in northern Spain. The fate of these men, many of them captured at Teruel or on the Ebro front was uncertain, for they could expect little sympathy from their Nationalist gaolers, now confident of victory and determined to eradicate the last vestiges of the Republic. In general, foreign nationals, if only due to the glare of international scrutiny, received better treatment than their Spanish comrades, but they were often forced to endure primitive living conditions and a severely restricted diet. Illness was to claim many victims in the prison camps while the shadow of summary court martial and execution hung continually over the British volunteers. In such circumstances the men eagerly awaited news of an exchange of prisoners or the intervention of a foreign power that might signal their release.

7

Prisoner-of-war

After nearly two years of active service I had come to accept the idea of my own death. It was something with which I had come to terms after seeing so many of my comrades cut down in battle. I was not, however, mentally prepared for the experience of being a prisoner-of-war. Never had I envisaged that I would be captured: killed, yes, but incarcerated in a prison, no. Yet I have to concede that being taken prisoner probably saved my life, since of the 377 men of the British Battalion who took up position at the front on the night of 22nd September only 173 were able to complete the withdrawal on the night of the 24th after the last action which the Battalion fought on Spanish soil.

If I was mentally unprepared for captivity I was equally unprepared for the interrogation to which I was subjected. Some distance behind the Fascist forward positions I was marched into a dilapidated building and brought face-to-face with a Nationalist officer who looked as though he was about to step out on to a parade ground. His uniform had clearly been tailor-made and his accoutrements gleamed from the hours of careful attention which had been lavished on them by his batman. His appearance left no doubt in my mind that he had been a regular army officer who had thrown in his lot with Franco. I am sure that his entire demeanour gave him an immediate psychological advantage over me, as I stood before him in my dirty, soiled uniform with the dust of the battlefield clinging to me. He asked me a lot of questions about where I had come from and how long I had been in Spain and I lied my head off. I lied about everything! I denied being a company commander and insisted that Bill Briskey was my officer; after all, how was my interrogator to know that poor Bill had been killed on the first day at Jarama? I was adamant: I had only just arrived in Spain. I had had the misfortune to be captured on my first day in action. Lie followed lie as I struggled to make each one compatible with the ones which had preceded it.

When we had all been subjected to interrogation we were put together under armed guard and, naturally, our sole topic of conversation was, 'What did he ask you?' It soon transpired that we had all been lying furiously. The trouble was that our fabricated stories had not synchronized. On two points, however, we had all agreed: none of us had ever touched a machine-gun, let alone fired one, and none of us was anything but a simple squaddie. 'An officer in the Republican forces? Me? Never.' One of my comrades had claimed never to have fired a shot at anyone in his entire life, just to have been the driver of a supply lorry.

'Where did you say you had left your lorry?' I asked him.

'I never thought of that,' he replied. 'Anyway no one asked me about where I was supposed to have dumped it.'

I think this goes to show just how unprepared all of us were for captivity. I am sure, however, that had my interrogator been able to discover either from me or from one of my comrades that I had been an officer then I would have been shot on the spot. No one mentioned my rank and I thought how wonderfully well my young troops, especially the Spanish boys, had conducted themselves, since, in the panic of being taken prisoner, it would have been so easy for one of them to let slip that I was his company commander, or give the information away to ingratiate himself with his interrogators.

By the time the interrogations were concluded it was starting to get dark and we were told that we were to be taken further away from the front. To ensure that we gave value for money to our captors, we were employed as stretcher-bearers to carry the Fascist wounded back to the first-aid posts which had been prepared in advance of their attack. There was no reason why we should not have been employed in this capacity; even under the terms of the Geneva Convention such use can legitimately be made of prisoners-of-war. Our duties as stretcher-bearers completed, we were marched under a light guard to Gandesa where we were put aboard a train for Zaragoza. A miserable overnight journey ended at first light as we disembarked on to the railway platform in the city which we had long striven to capture but which had always withstood our best efforts and remained firmly in the hands of the Fascists.

I would vehemently deny that I was in any way demoralized by being made a prisoner-of-war, but my spirits were lowered as I came to appreciate that the Republic now had not the slightest chance of securing victory over the Nationalists. When I saw at first-hand how well-fed and clothed the enemy troops were, when I saw the transport and weaponry at their disposal, I knew that the Fascists were certain to triumph. From

accounts which I have since read I now know that the political leaders of the Republic were thinking the same and were seriously considering negotiating a surrender of their forces, even with the knowledge that little mercy would be shown by the Fascists should a peace settlement result.

In one sense for me the war had already ended when I was captured, but in another sense it still continued, since I was now in enemy hands and, in the absence of a negotiated peace between the two protagonists, my safety was far from guaranteed. The true magnitude of my predicament was brought home to me at the railway station in Zaragoza when I was singled out from the other prisoners and taken to the military barracks, while the others were marched off under guard to the civilian prison. I never did learn why I was accorded this special treatment.

It was the silence which struck me most forcibly when the door of my cell clanged shut behind me. After days and nights of listening to the firing and explosion of heavy artillery shells, of being deafened and stunned by the incredible noise of modern warfare now I could hear only the sounds made by my own movements in the cramped confines of my cell. At first I was unnerved by such profound silence which seemed to suggest the presence of an alien and oppressive force, but gradually I adjusted to it and, even grew to like it as I learnt anew the pleasure of tranquillity.

My cell was very much the norm for prison cells. At some time it had been rudely furnished, but now only marks on the walls and floor showed where a bunk bed, a small table and a chair had once stood. A small, barred window set high up in one of the walls provided some natural light, but I had no means of reaching it to gain a view of the world outside. Above the door was a recess which housed a diminutive electric bulb which was screened with thick glass. This light burnt day and night and threw a miserable glow over the cell after sunset. Above the light was a large crucifix with the inevitable figure of Christ carved in relief upon it; but this representation of Christ had been 'doctored' to exhibit a political preference, for the loin-cloth was painted in the red and yellow stripes of Franco's Fascist movement. The cell lacked any bedding or floor-covering and as I wore only a khaki shirt and trousers and a pair of canvas shoes, the cold of the stone-floor struck through my clothes, and meant that I could not lie down to sleep but had to crouch with my back to a wall or wedge myself into a corner.

Over the next few days I was joined for a night or two by various companions, but all of them were Nationalist troops who had committed a vast range of minor misdemeanours, which had led to them being given a

brief taste of prison life. For two nights I shared my meagre accommodation with a Fascist from one of Franco's crack regiments. He took great exception to being made to share a cell with a member of the International Brigade, and resolutely refused to have anything to do with me. Whenever I tried to make conversation he simply turned his back on me and gazed intently at the wall. I decided to make the most of his stupidity and prattled away at him in English and Spanish for hour after hour; he must have come to know every crack and blemish of our cell walls intimately by the time he was released! I was also joined for a short time by an old Moorish soldier who proved a good deal more amicable but who, nevertheless, insisted on 'keeping his distance'.

The guard on my cell was changed every four hours, day and night. At each change the incoming guard opened the door of the cell and I had to spring to attention and stand before the wall furthest from the door. I then had to salute and say 'Franco'. If I was at all slow in responding the guard showed an uncontrollable inclination to speed up my reactions by kicking me. I was fed twice a day, once in the morning and again at dusk. Those who were locked up with me were taken from the cell each morning under guard, no doubt to perform menial functions in the barracks, but I was simply left to kick my heels and idle away the hours as best I could. I am inclined to think that those employed on fatigues probably qualified for an extra meal, because around midday the routine noise of barrack life fell away as though everyone else was eating.

Every morning on the barrack square outside my cell a general assembly would take place. A cultured voice, perhaps that of the Commandant, would recite details of the most recent Nationalist triumphs at the front and extol the virtues of life in Franco's Spain. This address was always concluded in the same manner with the speaker shouting '*España*', and there would be an answering roar of '*Una*'. Again the voice would call, '*España*' to which the rejoinder, '*Grande*', would echo out. A third cry of, '*España*' would elicit the response, '*Libre*'. Finally, the shout would be '*Arriba España*' which would be answered by '*Arriba España*'. A rendition of the Nationalist Anthem, '*Cara al Sol*', would then bring the morning's pep-talk to a conclusion.

The idea came to me that if I could fall in with a working party when it left the cell-block to begin its daily labour I might be able to find a way to escape. One morning I simply attached myself to the end of the line of such a party, only to be immediately spotted by a guard and roughly manhandled back into my cell. Undeterred I decided to attempt the same thing the next day, but this time I pushed into the middle of the line

hoping that I would thus be less conspicuous. This scheme also failed and I collected a few more cuts and bruises for my audacity.

One bright morning, with the light from an autumnal sun streaming through the bars of the cell-window, I was ordered by a Fascist sergeant to leave the cell. With him in front of me and with an armed guard falling into step on each side of me, I was taken across the parade-ground to the administration block. After a wait of a few minutes outside an office I was marched into a spacious room with a long table in its centre, at which sat some Fascist 'top brass'. In their beautifully tailored uniforms resplendent with épaulettes and medals they were an impressive sight. The sergeant approached the table with an exhibition of true military style and answered several questions put to him in a quiet voice by a man whom I took to be the most senior officer present. At one point the officer leant to his right to look round the sergeant and toward me. He scrutinized me carefully and I heard him say, 'Yes. There is no doubt. He is English.' The sergeant withdrew from the table and gave me the instruction, 'About turn, quick march'. I was taken back to my cell where the sergeant treated me to his understanding of the recently concluded proceedings with the immortal words, 'You've had it, comrade'. So, I had just attended my court-martial, and one which would surely have qualified as a contender for the fastest on record.

The fate of those who had received similar 'hearings' left me in no doubt that the sentence would be death by firing squad and I was left to wonder when the execution would be carried out. One thing was certain: I was not going to be allowed any right of appeal against the decision of the court. I was inclined to think that the evening of the next day would be the most likely time designated for my execution, and I began to steel myself to go to my death with as much dignity and defiance as I could summon. I slept little that night, and many of my thoughts were of my family whom I never expected to see again. Would they learn of my death or would they simply assume when many months had passed with no news of me reaching them that I died somewhere in Spain. Those thoughts troubled me far more than the imminence of my own demise for that, after all, was something tangible with which I could come to terms. At dusk a few days later the sergeant with his two-man escort again appeared at the door of my cell and ordered me to accompany him. If nothing else it looked as though I had accurately forecast the time of my execution! Now a sentence of death is supposed to concentrate the mind of the condemned most wondrously. No doubt the poor man is supposed to see episodes from his past flash before his eyes and to recall with regret missed

opportunities and the fact that he will never again be able to engage in activities from which he has derived pleasure. This did not happen to me! As I left my cell I was engaged in a titanic struggle to make my limbs operate and to stop my bowels from functioning. I was going to my death but I felt as though I was already well over three-quarters of the way there. Somehow I managed to pull myself together so that I was at least able to put one foot in front of the other, but I was convinced that my strong, defiant cry of '*Viva la Republica*' as I faced the firing-squad would come out as a hoarse whisper. It really looked as if the romantic exit from life which I had conceived in my cell was going to turn into a sad and rather ridiculous parody of what I had envisaged.

However, instead of being placed against a wall and asked if I had any last requests – can the condemned man really reply, 'Yes. Just one. Please don't shoot me.' – I was taken to the main gate of the barracks where a party of captured Republican soldiers were drawn up in marching order. I was told to take my place in the ranks and we were then led under heavy guard to the railway-station where we were ordered into a train made up of what were probably cattle-trucks; at least each truck had a sliding door, no fittings and an all-pervading smell of animal. Slowly the train wound its way through Aragon as we engaged in relating tales of our experiences in captivity and enjoyed the pleasure of being together again after our enforced separation. For hours the train trundled along until at last it reached Burgos where we were commanded to disembark, form ranks and march under guard to our still unknown destination. The march lasted several hours before ending at the village of San Pedro de Cardeña, a place famous throughout Spain because El Cid was buried in its Church.

Our place of captivity in San Pedro was a decaying palace. Years of neglect had transformed it and robbed it of its former splendours. Only the scale of its architecture gave any inkling as to its earlier grandeur. Now where there had doubtless been splendour and cleanliness there was decay and filth. Our presence did nothing to change things for the better for we prisoners stank to high heaven. I was still in the same uniform in which I had been taken prisoner and had not been given any opportunity during my captivity to change or wash my clothes, nor had I been issued with soap and towel. Space for us new arrivals had been created by an exchange of prisoners-of-war negotiated between the Nationalists and the Republic. Many of our men who had fallen into Fascist hands during the retreat through Aragon had been released and sent home to England in return for the freeing of an equal number of Italian troops held in Republican-controlled camps in Catalonia.

San Pedro was a terrible place. Each floor of the building seemed to have been knocked into one large room with perhaps one hundred or more men confined within it. There was no furniture, no chairs, no beds, just bare boards upon which we sat and slept, and no blankets in which to wrap ourselves at night or when the weather turned cold. The food was dreadful even by the standards which we had come to expect and accept. A wet concoction was served to us each morning. This delicacy, which could not have tried the imagination of the staff of the world's worst army cook-house, was basically tepid water with a few stale bread-crumbs floating on it, and with a touch of garlic added to give it some flavour. It was more of a drink than a meal. At midday we were served with a piece of bread and a few beans. The bread had to last for the rest of the day. At night we were offered a few more beans to eat with the carefully husbanded remains of the lunchtime bread. The menu, needless to say, never changed and never varied in either quality or quantity. So bad was the food and so lacking in nutrition that nearly all of the men who had been confined in San Pedro since their capture in the spring were covered in ulcers. Each hideous-looking ulcer had a loose blob on its upper surface below which was a pus-filled sac. I have since described these ulcers to a doctor who said that, although he could not be certain of the exact nature of the complaint without actually having seen the symptoms for himself, he was prepared to hazard a guess that they were caused by the prisoners having contracted the old seamen's disease of scurvy. What we would have given to have had a qualified doctor complete with medical supplies with us in San Pedro! As it was we had to make do with the rudimentary knowledge of one of our Polish comrades who had a few bandages and a pair of scissors. Occasionally, when a prisoner was especially badly afflicted by ulcers, our 'doctor' managed to prevail upon the camp commandant to have the man put on what we laughingly called a 'green diet'. This meant that the poor unfortunate would receive a supplement to his daily rations: a glass of milk, so watered down that it had a blue tinge to it, and a lettuce leaf. I cannot think that the milk did any good at all but the lettuce leaf seemed to bring about a slow if unspectacular improvement.

Although I was not at San Pedro long enough to suffer the worst effects of malnutrition, I did have occasion to use the services of our 'medic'. I managed to get a splinter from the floor deep into my hand and in the filthy conditions it quickly turned septic. My Polish comrade worked a miracle by lancing my hand with one of the blades of his scissors and removing the splinter. Luckily for me the wound stayed free of infection and healed.

We were confined to our quarters except at meal-times when we were permitted to go into the courtyard to collect our food. The absence of exercise and with so many men being cooped up in insanitary conditions with no washing facilities were factors which encouraged the spread of all kinds of diseases and lice had a field day. We were all alive with them. At night we stripped off all our clothes no matter how cold the weather because there was a partially proven theory that lice will leave cold clothes. The theory may have been basically sound but it did not always work to our satisfaction; but at least when we were naked we could see and feel the lice, catch them and then kill them by the simple expedient of squeezing them between thumb and finger.

San Pedro was a multi-national prison. I should think that there were men incarcerated within its walls from at least forty different countries. The largest contingent came from Portugal; so numerous were they that they occupied an entire wing of the building. Also they were the only inmates of San Pedro who were not prisoners-of-war but were migrant workers who had for generations entered Spain looking for work. Before the war they had been encouraged to enter the country and had even been deliberately brought in to act as strike-breakers. When crossings of the border between Spain and Portugal had become tightly controlled many of these transitory labourers had been trapped in Spain and as they had no permits authorizing them to be there they were imprisoned until such time as their own government would accept them back; something it was slow to do.

Escape from San Pedro was a recurring thought in many minds but successful escape attempts were seldom achieved. Before my arrival several such ventures had been attempted at a time when the prisoners were allowed to go to the stream in the nearby village to wash. This presented the best opportunity for captives to head off for the open fields, but those doing so inevitably found themselves in a hostile environment in which they could not obtain food or transport, and, unfailingly, they were recaptured and harshly beaten before being returned to the prison. Hardly surprisingly these escape attempts had led to increased vigilance by the guards and the confinement of the inmates to the prison itself. I know of only one escape attempt being made whilst I was at San Pedro and that was made by a Dutchman who, shortly before Christmas, had received some mail which had made him very homesick and he had resolved to make a break for freedom. Within forty-eight hours he was returned to the prison in a terrible state. His body was covered in cuts and bruises and one of his eyes was completely closed. His face was so badly

swollen that I did not at first recognize him and for days afterward he was in agony: every time he moved a fresh spasm of pain would cause his body to tense.

This hell-hole of a place was administered by the Spanish authorities, but they received plenty of 'advice' from the Gestapo. Frequently Gestapo personnel appeared on the scene and people would be taken away, ostensibly to be interviewed. I strongly suspect that in practice 'to be interviewed' meant to be put to death, for none of the interviewees ever reappeared. No one was shot at San Pedro – executions were always carried out at Burgos – but a number of men died in captivity, and this raised the question of burial services as the deceased were invariably atheists. Every day a Catholic priest and two nuns visited the prisoners, but they only received anything approaching a welcome from the Portuguese. However, the priest was clearly concerned and distressed by the current practice of throwing the bodies of the dead into a hole in the ground, even if the recently departed had had no time for him and his message, so he had prevailed upon the Spanish Commandant to provide a coffin for the corpse and gained permission to hold funeral services at the graveside. The Fascists soon found a way of cutting down on the cost of coffins for atheistic, foreign prisoners-of-war who had had the audacity to die in their care. As soon as a funeral service was over and the priest and his accompanying nuns had departed the guards would remove the body from the coffin, drop it into the grave, cover it with earth and return with the coffin which would be put in store ready for its next unfortunate occupant. I have no idea who paid for the original coffin but if our clerical friends were being charged for a new coffin for each funeral then someone was doing very nicely at the expense of church funds!

An incident which involved me at San Pedro and which gave me food for thought occurred in November 1938. When I had first been taken prisoner, I had changed my identity and assumed my mother's maiden name, Wright. As the Spanish cannot pronounce the letter 'W' whenever my name was called out it always sounded like 'Righty' or some variation along those lines. On arrival at San Pedro I had been assured that a representative of the British Government made occasional visits to the prison and that I could safely revert to the use of my proper name. So it was under the name of Gregory and with some trepidation that I was summoned to the office of the Spanish Commandant.

My anxiety was unfounded, for the Commandant simply asked me my name and enquired if I was keeping well. Given the conditions at San Pedro that question seemed very much out of place, but I replied that I

was fine; whereupon I was dismissed from my captor's presence. An unofficial camp committee had been established by the prisoners and I reported my experience to it. Did this sudden interest in my welfare bode well or ill for my future safety? Did it, for instance, suggest that the sentence passed on me by the Court Martial at Zaragoza was about to be enacted, or did it mean that that sentence of death, which still hung over me like a great black cloud, was about to be commuted? I simply had no idea. One of my fellow captives, an American who seemed most knowledgeable about the machinations of San Pedro's administration, assured me that I had nothing to fear, and that in his estimation I had been summoned to the Commandant simply because family and friends back home had been making enquiries about me. Later I learnt that this was so. My mother, having received no letters from me for several months, had lost a little of her legendary composure and had contacted her local Member of Parliament, Arthur Hayday, but he had shown neither sympathy nor understanding of her anxiety. Friends had suggested to her that she might be well advised to write to Willie Gallacher. After all, he had stayed at our house when speaking in Nottingham and, given his political persuasion, might prove more sympathetic and certainly more helpful. This mother had done, and Willie had taken up my case with the Foreign Office, which in turn had contacted the British representative in Spain who, for his part, had raised the question of my welfare with the Fascist authorities.

My third consecutive Christmas in Spain was spent in the squalor of San Pedro but, surprisingly, it was a more festive occasion than the two which had preceded it. On the morning of Christmas Day we were paraded in the courtyard for a religious service; indeed, attendance at religious services was very much a feature of prison life. The mass was in Latin and the order of service was something with which very few of us were familiar. We always seemed to be standing when we should have been kneeling and vice-versa. The guards did their best to instil the correct form of observance into us by using the butts of their rifles to make us assume the appropriate posture. Under this far from subtle education process we proved remarkably adept pupils, but none of us felt inclined to be converted. What made Christmas Day special for us was the arrival of a lorry containing boxes of chocolates, Spanish cigarettes, and gifts from charitable bodies at home. I was given three bars of chocolate and a couple of packets of cigarettes, which I promptly exchanged for another two chocolate bars, and a book of English poetry. Now a book of verse may seem a strange thing to send as a gift to a man languishing in a Fascist gaol,

but I thoroughly enjoyed reading the poems. Over the weeks that followed I read them so often that I can still recite many of them word-perfect after nearly fifty years. Inside the front cover of the book was a short dedication which read, 'With Best Wishes from the Society of Friends'. In the evening, with the approval of the Commandant, we staged a concert. Without his permission the concert would have been impossible, so he had to be invited despite our hatred of him. He took the place of honour in the front row where he sat in splendid isolation with his senior staff seated in the row behind him. Differences of rank were clearly important in the Fascist forces, and obviously had to be observed on all occasions. Having no stage talent whatsoever I was not directly involved in the singing, dancing or the short play which passed as a skit of camp life. From time to time the Commandant forced a frigid smile to his lips and we all enjoyed his contrived good humour and his stilted and reluctant attempts to enter into the spirit of things. As I closed my eyes that night I felt that I had had a wonderful day. I had filled myself with chocolate and laughed helplessly at the intended and unintended comedy of the concert. For a few precious hours the misery of captivity had been swept away.

Such an escape from the monotony of a miserable existence was unique. For the most part boredom pressed down upon us like a huge weight. Occasionally camp meetings took place under the watchful eyes of the guards and each of those meetings ended with a rousing rendition of the British Battalion's song, 'There's a Valley in Spain called Jarama'. We belted it out at the tops of our voices with everyone on his feet standing to attention, heads up, shoulders back. We did not dare to sing the much better known, 'Internationale' for fear of incurring the wrath of our lords and masters. Numerous discussion groups were established but these tended to become rather sterile affairs after a while as we were starved of information about events in the outside world. Such news as did reach us had invariably been manipulated and reformulated by the guards, who were our sole contact with life beyond the walls, and was calculated to lower our spirits rather than to raise them.

Sometimes, when the Fascists had secured what they considered to be a major military victory in the war which was still raging many miles away from the prison, we would be assembled in the courtyard to hear of the glorious triumphs of the Nationalist armed forces. A sergeant was given the task of finding one native speaker from each of the national groups drawn up on parade to read the glad tidings to his comrades. We made the most of such events. Not one of us was English: Welsh, Scottish, Irish, yes, but English, never. The sergeant would then dutifully report to the

Commandant that there were no Englishmen present and the Commandant would throw a fit. 'English, Welsh, Scottish, Irish they are all the same,' he would yell as his face turned purple, and the veins in his forehead bulged. Although we could fool a poor, uneducated sergeant we could not fool the Commandant, and after enjoying this game a couple of times it became boring and we abandoned it. The news that was read out on those occasions was, to say the least, far-fetched. The demise of entire Republican divisions was broadcast, whilst tens of thousands of prisoners had been allegedly taken by Franco's forces, to say nothing of the destruction of several armoured brigades and the loss to the Republic of hundreds of aircraft. If propaganda is to have the desired effect it has to be credible, and we treated these preposterous claims as jokes. If they were to be believed, then the Fascists were shooting down the entire Republican air force on an almost daily basis. Doubtless they were meeting with a good deal of success in the field, but not even the Fascists could shoot down all of our planes every day of the week.

The most popular way to isolate ourselves from the daily horror of life in the filth of San Pedro was to play chess. Chess-sets were not provided for us but had to be made. Some of the lads had noticed that the guards threw used razor-blades on to the rubbish-tip. These were stealthily retrieved and brought back to the dormitory where we fashioned chessmen from small sticks. Chess is a wonderful game to play in prison. It demands one's complete attention and can take several hours before victory is achieved, and in captivity time is plentiful and distractions are few. Under instruction from a few extremely able devotees of the game we all took it up with an enthusiasm bordering on the fanatical. I remember one of our Polish comrades who was so expert that he would play a dozen of us at once and invariably he would win every game. He consistently made mince-meat of me. I have no idea of how many times I played him, but I think that he never needed more than about ten moves before I found myself checkmated.

One night in early January as I made my way to the lavatory I chanced to look through the bars of a large window into the courtyard below. There a guard, with measured tread, was walking slowly to and fro and on the spur of the moment I worked a piece of stone loose from the decaying surround of the window and hurled it at him. It missed its intended target, but not by much, and bounced away across the yard. Unfortunately for me another guard whose presence I had not detected must have caught sight of my dirty, naked body outlined at the window, and he shot at me. Now it takes a lot of luck and a lot of experience to hit a target in the dark, especially

when there is no time in which to take careful aim. That second guard had both luck and experience on his side because, before I could move back into the darkness of the corridor, a bullet struck the ceiling above my head. I raced back to the dormitory and lay on the floor pretending to be asleep. Within minutes there was the sound of running footsteps and raised voices and the lights were turned on. Covered by the guns of an entire platoon of guards, we were made to stand to attention and a sergeant and the guard who had fired at me went off to the window to pick up the body. Of course there was no body to be found, not even a trace of blood, but we could all hear the guard repeating over and over again that he had definitely shot someone. A roll call was taken and when it revealed that all of the prisoners were accounted for, the sergeant started to yell abuse at the poor guard who still maintained that, despite all evidence to the contrary, he had scored a direct hit. The Commandant then appeared – in a foul temper at having had his sleep disturbed. He paced up and down the rows of assembled prisoners and when he was in front of me he stopped and stared at me hard and long. He pushed his face so close to mine that I could smell the tobacco and wine on his breath. He continued to stare at me, eye-ball to eye-ball, for what seemed like ages, before continuing his inspection. With that done, he gave the sergeant a real dressing-down and the sergeant then added a few choice phrases of his own to the rollicking he passed on to the guard who, by this time, was reduced to apologizing for everything.

Eventually we were left in peace and as we settled down I said to one of my comrades, 'Why d'you think that the Commandant stared at me like that?'

'I don't know,' he replied, 'but you are covered in brick dust, aren't you?'

Within a few days of that silly escapade we British were marched from the prison back to Burgos, and there we were loaded into a train made up of cattle-trucks, and despatched to San Sebastian and Ondaretta prison. San Sebastian had been the holiday resort of the Spanish Royal Family and had remained a very middle-class town. That much was obvious as we marched from the railway-station to our new place of confinement. In front of our column there was a loudspeaker van which was informing the local populace that General Franco had, through his generosity, decided to release the misguided foreigners who had now come to see the error of their ways and were anxious to make recompense for the crimes which they had committed against Spain and the Spanish people. A real load of rubbish, but one which clearly struck a sympathetic chord with the well-

dressed, well-fed bourgeoisie of San Sebastian who lined the streets to hurl abuse at us as we passed. We tried to look anything but meek and guilt-ridden. One particularly sturdy and prosperous-looking woman took an instant dislike to me as I passed in front of her, for she ran alongside and battered me with her umbrella, until a guard stopped her. The middle-class supporters of Fascism were, however, not the only ones thronging the pavements in the town centre. There were a lot of working-class people who made an especially pathetic sight as they held up photographs of fathers, sons, husbands and brothers who had gone to fight for the Republic. They asked if we had seen their loved ones but we just had to shake our heads and say, 'No. Sorry. I've not seen him. I hope he returns soon.' It was a heartbreaking experience because doubt and anxiety were written all over the faces of the questioners. Although they felt that they had to ask, it was clear that all of them feared the answer they might receive.

Except for the presence of the British prisoners-of-war, Ondoretta prison was exclusively for Spanish civilians, and was still being run by its pre-war staff. Free of the ever-watchful eye of the Fascist military, we had a far better lifestyle here than we had known at San Pedro. We were allowed to leave our cells at regular intervals to take exercise in the prison yard. We walked round and round that yard for mile after mile and used this opportunity to regain some of our former fitness. This, and an improvement in our diet, soon produced a sense of well-being which we had almost forgotten. We were also allowed to talk with other prisoners, the majority of whom were Basques and Asturians. I would think that roughly half of Ondaretta's Spanish inmates had been subjected to some sort of court-martial and of those approximately half again had been sentenced to death either by firing-squad or garrotting. It was by no means unusual for a prisoner not to know that the death sentence had been passed on him until a priest arrived at the door of his cell to give him the last rites of the church. Many of those with whom I spoke thought that I had been very privileged to have been present at my own court martial in Zaragoza as they had not had the chance to attend their own. So much for Fascist justice which was neither done nor seen to be done.

8

Freedom

Our stay in Ondaretta lasted a month. Then, one morning, to our surprise the sixty men of the British Battalion were taken to the gatehouse and asked to put a thumbprint on their release papers. Carefully watched and shepherded by members of the Civil Guard, we were taken by train to the bridge at Irun on the French-Spanish border. One of the Civil Guards, resplendent in his shiny, black pork-pie hat with what appeared to be a bow of the same material attached to the back of it, stepped smartly out on to the bridge and marched purposefully to its exact mid-point where he executed a very precise 'halt'. We followed his example as none of us fancied being left behind in Spain when France was so invitingly close. As we walked past the guard, he quietly said, '*Adios*. God be with you.' I just could not resist replying, '*Adios, Hasta la Vista*'. Had I known then that it would be forty-two years before I next set foot on Spanish soil, I might not have been quite so arrogant. A few strides carried us into France and into freedom!

That day was surely one of the greatest of my life. I simply cannot convey all the feelings and emotions which I experienced: Relief at having come safely through the dangers of war, joy at being on my way home, excitement at the prospect of seeing my family again, sorrow over the certain defeat of the Republic, anger that the Fascists had been allowed to triumph because of the timidity and dual standards of the western democracies, and deep sadness at the loss of so many of my friends and comrades who would never be leaving Spain but lying for the rest of time in shallow graves in her dusty soil. All of these emotions and others welled up inside me, but no regret at having committed myself to a cause which I felt to be a just one. Then I was in France.

Without a word of command being given we automatically formed into marching order, we picked up step from the front, we swung our arms, raised our heads and spontaneously began to sing 'The Internationale'. A large crowd of French people lined the road on the other side of the

bridge, and as we passed through it we burst into a rendition of 'It's a Long Way to Tipperary', a song well-known in France and one which still had strong emotional appeal there at that time. We may not have sung well but we received a great cheer for our efforts. Under an escort drawn from the local gendarmerie we were taken to a building, perhaps a large school, where a party of nuns took our filthy clothes from us and where we underwent a thorough de-lousing process and a rudimentary medical examination. The ecstasy of soap and warm water! We were issued with new civilian clothes, which we were told had been paid for by the British Government, and after a hot meal we were on a special train and heading for Calais. In each carriage of the train was a French soldier complete with rifle, but he made no pretence of guarding us and within a few minutes of the journey starting our *poilu* had settled himself in a seat and placed his rifle on the luggage rack above his head.

News of our arrival must have spread throughout the entire French railway network for at every signal-box and station, railwaymen would stand and give us the clenched fist salute. Our elation at being free again sustained us all the way back to Dover where we were greeted by Joe Hincks, who had commanded the British Battalion during the battle of Brunete. A huge crowd awaited us at Victoria Station. There was shouting and singing, the noise was tremendous. My mother and younger sister had come down from Nottingham to meet me, and it was with them that I travelled home, trying hard to answer the thousand and one questions which they had stored up against the day of my return. It was a little over two years since they had last seen me and they wanted to know of all of my exploits during that time as fast as I could recount them. It was only when I stepped from the train on to the platform at Nottingham that I became conscious of just how sick and exhausted I felt. The long journey from Spain and the exhilaration of experiencing freedom must have used up the last vestiges of stamina. The remaining few miles home to Bulwell seemed an interminable ordeal and I sank into my bed with a sense of great relief and of almost unbearable weariness.

In prison I had tried to close my eyes to the grime and squalor which threatened to engulf me. I had eaten appalling food, no matter how revolting it had looked and tasted. At every turn I had been sustained by thoughts of the creature comforts of home and of the meals I would enjoy when I finally returned to Bulwell. Many times I planned my ideal day. I

would climb out of a warm bed after the pleasure of an undisturbed night's sleep between clean, white, linen sheets. I would wash and shave in warm, soapy water and then breakfast on cereal followed by a big plate of bacon, eggs and tomato accompanied by a veritable mountain of piping hot buttered toast, a feast which would be washed down with copious quantities of strong tea. This self-indulgent gluttony would see me through to 'elevenses' of coffee and biscuits which would itself be a forerunner to lunch. The rest of my ideal day continued in similar vein with food providing the central theme. Yet now I was at home I encountered only bitter disappointment for such a lavish diet proved far beyond the capacity of my stomach, even if money had been available to purchase such food.

It was only now that I came to appreciate fully just how hard a time my mother and sister had experienced during my voluntary absence, and I felt some pangs of guilt for having left them so financially impoverished. My mother had borne the trials of daily existence with customary fortitude and had never ceased to believe but that I would return to her safe and sound even after she had heard of Bernard's death at Teruel. My sister however, had been ill for long periods. She and I had been very close throughout our childhood and she had worried about me greatly especially when there had been long gaps between my letters home.

My friends in Nottingham did not seem to appreciate just how ill I was, both physically and mentally, after my discharge from prison. Nor did they understand the daunting task which faced me in learning to re-adjust to civilian life.

I received no hero's welcome back in Bulwell, nor had I expected one. In the East Midlands, as in the rest of Britain, people had turned their backs on Spain and were now preparing for another war. I felt some pressure to throw myself into this national effort and I knew many of my close friends expected me to commit myself to it, but I simply did not possess the strength to share in their endeavours. (When, eventually, I had to register for military service, I joined the Royal Navy.) But now there was the pressing search for work, and after a period on the dole at seventeen shillings and sixpence a week, and a temporary job at Nottingham Co-op, I found work as a clerk with the newly founded Nottingham Retail Meat Agents: a government organization established to enforce the new meat-rationing regulations.

One day, while sitting at my desk, I received a visitor. Bernard Winfield, my close friend who had been killed at Teruel, had been the son of a local butcher. On a regular visit to the slaughter-house Bernard's father had

Harry Pollitt speaking to the British Battalion on one of his visits to Spain

Willie Gallacher MP with two officers from the
British Battalion in Spain

THE Under-Secretary of State for Foreign Affairs presents his compliments to *Mr T. W. Gregory,* and, with reference to the letter from this Office of *June 24,* is directed by the Secretary of State to request that *he* will repay as soon as possible the sum of £ 3. - . 1, representing expenditure advanced from public funds by *his Majesty's Consul at Bordeaux,* in connection with *his* repatriation.

    The amount in question should be forwarded either by crossed cheque or crossed postal order payable to "The Finance Officer, Foreign Office."

Foreign Office,
    July 31 , 1940.

[Over

325 a

1916 A 20115—2

The Foreign Office's request for reimbursement for Walter's repatriation from Franco's prison. The bill remains unpaid.

heard that a lad who had fought in Spain was now working in the office, so Mr Winfield decided there and then to call in and have a chat with someone who might have known his youngest son. Would I call at his home to talk to his wife, he asked, as she was still dreadfully upset by Bernard's death. With much trepidation I agreed to visit them one evening after work. Mrs Winfield sat in an armchair with George standing behind her, and after a cup of tea I was subjected to a barrage of questions from the poor lady that only a mother could ask.

'Did Bernard have a nice coffin? Were there flowers on the grave? What was the headstone like? Who conducted the service? Were all of Bernard's friends able to come to pay their respects?'

I had not been prepared for questions such as these. Bernard had been buried at the height of a ferocious battle. There had been no time or materials to make a coffin, no opportunity for a burial service, no flowers grew in the snows of Teruel and Bernard's comrades were too busy fighting for their own lives to be able to attend a funeral service, had there even been one. I could not bring myself to tell the poor, grieving woman the realities of life in action and invented for her solace a truly memorable funeral. Pity, embarrassment and guilt all combined to make that evening a terrible one and it was with a tremendous sense of relief that I left their house, and rushed to the nearest pub for a few stiff drinks before going home to spend a sleepless night.

* * *

The Spanish Civil War ended with the surrender of Madrid on 28 March 1939. Despite the valour and heroism displayed over a period of three years the Republic collapsed in confusion and disarray in the early months of 1939 when it was apparent that Britain and France had no intention of rendering direct assistance to the Republican cause. Franco exploited the situation to the full by demanding unconditional surrender and refusing any form of amnesty for those who had supported the Republic. Forced into a corner, the various political factions within the Republican coalition fought out one last bitter and bloody battle amongst themselves on the streets of Madrid before finally surrendering to the Nationalist forces.

For Walter, and those who joined him in fighting for the Spanish Republic, what had started as a marvellous adventure had turned quickly into the grim reality of a protracted and brutal civil war with

death stalking the British Battalion at every turn. If, however, their vision of an heroic war was somewhat tarnished by the battlefields of Spain and the political feuding of the various Republican factions, the anti-Fascist cause, which had led to their original enlistment, remained as a source of inspiration throughout the conflict. The camaraderie of the Battalion and the faith in their purpose transcended the horrors of war and bound the volunteers together in admiration for both the Spanish people and the ultimate justice of their cause. Sam Wild spoke for the entire Battalion when, upon their return to Britain, he declared that although the Civil War was apparently lost they would nevertheless continue the fight against Fascism.

9

Why did I go to fight in Spain?

Questioners seem surprised when I can offer no ready answer. In truth, there is no ready answer to offer. I went not because one event decided me to do so, but because it seemed the natural, even the right thing to do. It was, quite simply, the culmination of my experiences up until that time that made me accept Clarence Mason's invitation. I have never regretted doing so. Sam Wild once said to me that after Spain his life was never the same. I have to agree, but I am at a loss to explain the difference in me wrought by my experience of fighting Fascism. I simply know that the Spanish Civil War changed the world, and it also most certainly changed me and the way in which I viewed the world.

My childhood ought to have been a time of enjoyment and laughter, of eager exploration of an unknown and enticing world. For many of my generation, growing up in the years between the end of the Edwardian era and the outbreak of the First World War, such an optimistic view was in stark contrast to the realities of our young lives.

I was born in Lincoln, a city noted for its magnificent cathedral: it dominates the town and is surrounded by the houses of Lincoln's more prosperous citizens. Lytton Street, where I entered the world, did not enjoy such an elevated position either geographically or socially, being down in the valley among the factories where the majority of Lincoln's working-class lived. I became conscious of this distinction at a very early age. I knew that I belonged down the hill, and nothing that happened in my childhood led me to believe that I was entitled to think of myself as being in any way equal to those who dwelt in the fashionable houses on the hillside above.

Lytton Street was probably no better and no worse than many streets in working-class districts in other towns in Britain. It was a street of small terraced houses of the 'two-up-two-down' variety. The fumes and noise of the factories lay heavily around but my parents could afford no other home. My mother and father were not Lincoln people: they were from

Newark, and my father had been obliged to move his young family to Lincoln when he had at last found work there. It is all too easily forgotten that unemployment was a problem in the years before the Great War, but for all too many working-class people the horror and stigma of life without work coloured their existence and conditioned their every thought, long before the miseries of war with Germany were added to their already heavy burden.

It would be wrong of me now to attribute blame to anyone for the austerity of my early life. Certainly my parents did all they could to make our existence as pleasant as possible, but they were faced by insuperable difficulties in securing even the smallest of luxuries. Today it is hard to realize just what hardship the working-class people endured as the world moved toward the Great War. In many parts of Lincoln children could be seen running around the streets in bare feet, not only before the war but long after it was over and Lloyd George's 'land fit for heroes' failed to materialize.

On arriving in Lincoln from Newark my father found work as a carpenter with a firm of agricultural machinery specialists, so our plight was far less serious than that of many of our immediate neighbours. Because of the unprecedented demands made on industry by the First World War much of their work was switched from peace-time production to the manufacture of war material. As specialists in building in wood, their production was channelled into making gun carriages and aircraft wings which bore a close resemblance to a cycle frame with wooden struts, and which were then covered with canvas. Unfortunately, by the end of the war, the firm had not only lost touch with its pre-war customers but its particular skills had been largely overtaken by technological advances and although it struggled on until about 1930, it was never able to achieve its previous profitability.

Our relative prosperity permitted my parents to move from the house they rented in Lytton Street to another rented property in Bernard Street. This move meant little real change in our living conditions for, although we now had a third bedroom, the basic amenities remained much as before. The lavatory was outside and in winter there was a loathing to leave the warmth of the kitchen to undertake the dark and cold journey across the yard. As a boy I must have spent many hours on miserable winter evenings sitting by the grate with legs tightly crossed and squirming about uncomfortably trying to delay as long as possible the inevitable rush across the unlit yard. We bathed in a zinc tub on the hearth, and the fact that the house was built into the hillside meant that at

the first onset of winter the wallpaper at the bottom of the damp walls hung loose and billowed about in the draught whenever a door was opened.

Yet compared to many of our immediate neighbours we were favoured, not simply by the relative prosperity which we enjoyed because of my father's regular employment, but also because we were spared the worst excesses of the First World War. Father was in a protected occupation, but I think his health, which had never been good, would have rendered him ineligible for military service. The fact that my father was never away from home during the Great War meant that his influence upon me was strong.

One of my earliest recollections was of just before the end of the war when there was a Zeppelin raid on Lincoln. As the drone of the airship's engines grew louder with its approach people ran from their houses to some nearby allotments. Why they should have done this has often puzzled me, since they would have been far safer had they remained at home. Bombing raids in the First World War, particularly against civilian targets, were not sophisticated. In the old airships the engines had to be stopped in order to aim the bombs, which were then heaved over the side by hand. It would seem that the Zeppelin had followed a train along the main line from the south into Lincoln. Once it was realized, a signalman had instructions to stop the train, in a cutting very close to our house, to prevent extensive bomb damage to the centre of the city. So primitive was the art of bomb-aiming that neither the train nor any of the built-up area in the immediate neighbourhood was hit, as the bombs fell harmlessly in the surrounding open countryside. I vividly remember the screech of the falling bombs and the crunch and flash they made upon impact, but my first experience of aerial bombardment held none of the terrors which it was later to assume. So novel was this bombing that the next day all of us local children went out into the nearby fields and began an intensive search in the now water-filled bomb-craters for pieces of shrapnel which we quickly sold as souvenirs for a penny or two pence.

If my early days were lacking in luxuries, and on occasions things which today are taken as necessities, they were not lacking in a certain degree of uniformity. Both of my parents were non-conformists (I was christened at Walmer Street Chapel in Lincoln), both of them shopped at the local co-operative store. This was essential to my mother's attempts to balance the family budget, for without the quarterly dividend not only ourselves, but countless thousands like us, would have had to go without the little extras like children's shoes or a coat. If the chapel and the co-op produced two

elements of continuity in my childhood, the third was my father's commitment to the trade union movement. Since serving his apprenticeship as a carpenter, my father had been a member of the Woodworkers' Union and whilst union membership had not led him to join a political party there was no doubt but that his political allegiance lay with the Labour Party. Even before I was old enough to go to school my Dad would take me to meetings organized by the Conservative Party at which he would heckle the speakers.

My school career proved uneventful and almost devoid of distinction in any field of academic endeavour. I failed the entrance examination to Lincoln Technical College and the only tangible result of my educational efforts until the age of fourteen, when I left school, was a silver medal which I won in an exhibition in which I entered a table with a rather ornate inlaid top. Although I still have the medal the table has long since disappeared. Looking back it seems somewhat ironic that the single most rewarding experience of my school years was to prove of little value when I began to look for work just after the General Strike of 1926, for by then there were literally no prospects of securing any form of work in the woodwork trade. Even if there had been any, my father's experiences would not have encouraged me. He had left his old firm and had found another employer. At that time of slack orders and a plentiful supply of labour it became accepted practice for firms to set men on to complete a particular order and to stand them off when the order had been met. The work force thus became dependent on new orders being secured and endured frequent bouts of unemployment. Dad fell foul of his new employer when, with the completion of an order, he was about to be stood off. The men working on the order had been paid on piece-work and under a union agreement were entitled to payment for time spent in sharpening tools as well as for the number of pieces of work they had completed. Dad alone sought payment for the time he had spent in preparing his tools. His request was met with a curt refusal and he was told that if he were to persist in his demand he would be blacklisted by the company. Being pig-headed and feeling that he was being cheated of what was rightly his under the union agreement, he continued to argue his case. The outcome was inevitable, not only did he not receive the money he was seeking, but he was blacklisted, which in practice meant that all of the firms in and around Lincoln which were members of the local employers' federation refused to employ him. He never really worked again, and such jobs as he did have were of short duration with firms not belonging to the federation. As though to compound the felony, Dad's health which had

been far from good for a number of years became progressively worse. He was frequently afflicted by severe back-ache, caused by the onset of Bright's Disease.

For a short time while I was still at school we lived on unemployment and sickness benefit, the one replacing the other with almost monotonous regularity. Unemployment benefit was payable only to those 'genuinely seeking work' and like so many thousands of others Dad was caught up in the time-consuming practice of showing up at factory gates to ask for work, for only by doing so could he answer the inevitable question, 'Where have you been today in search of work?' The 'genuinely seeking work' stipulation did not, fortunately, prevail for too long. For it proved equally unpopular with management who found their offices and factories surrounded by large crowds seeking work which both employers and unemployed knew was simply not there to be had. Nor was our financial situation improved by Mother being unable to find work despite her willingness. At that time there was little work in Lincoln for women: there were a few hotels which employed female domestics, a small sweet factory which perhaps had a work-force of twenty to thirty girls, and there was some work to be had for shop assistants. I therefore looked upon it as my good fortune when, almost immediately after leaving school, I found a clerical job at the princely wage of eight shillings a week. In addition I found an evening job delivering prescriptions, either by bicycle or on foot, for a local doctor. For this I was paid seven shillings and sixpence per week, which virtually doubled my income. I must have been a very well-paid part-time delivery-boy for I could not have worked for Dr Derbyshire for more than four evenings a week, as I attended night-school three times a week during term-time, studying shorthand one night, bookkeeping another and, if I recall correctly, English on the third.

Night classes were very popular in those days, as they were the only means of career advancement. Despite my efforts, however, the family finances remained precariously balanced, with the threat of unpaid bills and unmet needs being carefully weighed against a small and cherished income.

Life is full of ironies and it has always seemed to me ironic that Dad's death in 1930, if anything, improved our financial situation and tilted the balance a little away from the red and a little toward the black. Dad's death meant that my mother now received a widow's pension which, although probably amounting to under a pound a week, together with the few shillings which she received for my younger sister, Kathleen, and added to the money I was bringing home, produced a degree of certainty, if not

security, where money was concerned, which we had not known for several years. Also my elder sister, Edith, had left home and gone to Nottingham where she had found work in domestic service. Our affluence was of course relative, as our total income can rarely have exceeded two pounds in any one week, but thanks to the good offices of friends my mother found occasional domestic work in an hotel, which eventually led to her working outside Lincoln and 'living-in'. This left me to look after the house and my younger sister who was still at school. Hotel pay was extremely poor with most of the staff being dependent upon tips to supplement their low wages, but Mother never found work in an hotel where the tips amounted to much, and, although she sent home as much money as she could, the family fortunes were in absolute terms meagre.

It was whilst I was working as a clerk that I joined a trade union for clerical workers. In the wake of the collapse of the General Strike and for a number of years to follow, there was a tremendous anti-union feeling among employers, and perhaps it was because of this obvious hostility in a period when there was little work that the Lincoln branch of the union had but a handful of members and never held meetings. I used to go and pay my subscription to a man who was looking after the one branch that existed in Lincoln. He worked as a clerk in a solicitor's office and apparently his employer did not object to me calling in occasionally to pay my union dues. Although I knew the union branch to be totally ineffective, my joining was not simply an act of defiance in the face of anti-union sentiment, but was a natural development from my own pro-union family background. It also accorded well with what I had seen, during my last year at school, of the response in Lincoln to the General Strike and with my sympathy for the strikers. At that time in 1926 my father was enjoying one of his spasmodic periods of employment on a small private job and did not dare to be seen walking to work with his tool-bag, but had to stuff the tools he was likely to need during that day into various pockets, and this precaution had to be taken despite the fact that the woodworkers had not been called out on strike. The event which was guaranteed to elicit the greatest outward emotion in Lincoln during the General Strike was not the presence of the occasional man surreptitiously making his way along the road to work, but the convoy of lorries which passed through the city carrying fruit and vegetables to Covent Garden market in London. These convoys provided a ready target for the hail of stones which inevitably greeted them from the ranks of striking workers who had assembled to show their displeasure at such strike-breaking activity. Even police protection failed to deter the strikers from their purpose, but did ensure

that the lorries reached their destination despite the missiles which were directed at them, often with great force and accuracy and always in great number.

In the years immediately following the General Strike it did not require a tremendous amount of intelligence to foresee the hardships which were to lie ahead. The Wall Street Crash in 1929 was but a dramatic pointer to the economic crisis which was daily becoming more apparent and the misery that this failure of capitalism would bring to untold millions in the western industrialized world. Increasingly I became aware that even my lowly clerical position was under threat and I began to answer job adverts in the *Lincolnshire Echo*. Nor did I restrict myself to clerical jobs, for these were monopolized by boys with a grammar-school education: an education far in excess of any which I possessed, even with regular attendance at night school. In 1932 the moment which I dreaded arrived: I was made redundant.

Armed with my last pay-packet and a far from ungracious testimonial I began to look for new employment with vigour. No longer did I apply for jobs by letter, now I walked from shop to shop, factory to factory, knowing that come Friday there would be no pay packet nestling reassuringly in my jacket pocket. Like thousands of others I would have taken any job offered no matter how menial, but like thousands of others no offers came my way. The employment situation in Lincoln was dreadful.

During this period of enforced idleness I first became politically aware, although my political consciousness had undoubtedly been roused by memories of the General Strike and the campaigns leading up to the 1931 general election. I can still remember the election posters and the appeals to vote for the National Government as the only means of safeguarding jobs. I recall the waving of Deutschmarks on political platforms and the threat that failure to lend support to Ramsay MacDonald would lead to inflation in Great Britain on the horrendous scale it had assumed in Germany, and that many more jobs would disappear as a result. Yet my abiding memory is of the hostility toward MacDonald which existed among the working-class supporters of the Labour Party. When I first became aware of the Labour Party, all the staunch party members had a photograph of MacDonald on the mantelpiece – to many he was virtually a god. In forming a National Government he betrayed those people.

My first political action was moderate by any stretch of the imagination: I joined the Labour Party League of Youth. I did so, not because a radical fire had been lit within me, although such a fire had begun to smoulder in my resentment at being out of work with little prospect of being in work in

the foreseeable future. It was simply part of a natural progression. I had, after all, been brought up in a home which gave its support to the Labour Party and the Co-operative movement, which read the *Daily Herald* and had a commitment to the trade union movement. Such was my political naïveté that I did not appreciate that I had joined an organization which was truly more active in the social field than it ever was in the political arena. Despite this it did furnish me with a route which was to lead to increased political awareness. Perhaps of greater moment, however, was the decision which I took to attend classes organized by the Workers Education Association, rather than simply idle away the empty hours of unemployment. I had long been aware of my educational limitations and had tried to overcome these through night school and now through courses run by the WEA, and it was these which set the political blood flowing through my veins.

The WEA in Lincoln was run by a lady called Miss Cameron who had a real interest in the difficulties which working-class people were encountering. So much so that Miss Cameron even tried to run workshops for the unemployed. Her commitment was reflected in many of the courses which I attended: on the current state of British political and economic life, on the Soviet Union, on the role that government could play in the economic field, and even on the writings of Karl Marx, although I have to admit that I found the latter particularly hard-going with my all-too-limited educational background. What a contrast I found between school and the WEA! At school education came a poor second to discipline. No doubt this was partly due to the man who was my headmaster throughout my school years. He was possessed of a strong personality and imprinted his views most forcibly upon all of his pupils' day-to-day activities. A prominent non-conformist and at one time president of the Lincoln Co-operative Society, he was a thorough-going disciplinarian. It was perhaps typical of him that not having set eyes upon me for the best part of ten years he should write to me while I was in the trenches at Jarama. In his letter, the only one I ever received from him, he expressed his hopes that I would come safely through the Civil War and instructed me in no uncertain terms that I should not waste such a golden opportunity to learn Spanish! As I never became fluent in Spanish, but gained only sufficient proficiency to meet my immediate needs, I suppose I would have incurred his wrath had we ever met again. Compared with the rigidity of the school régime and its authoritarian leader, the WEA placed great emphasis upon opening its students' minds and sought to develop their analytical faculties.

After twelve months without any form of work whatsoever I enjoyed a little good fortune. My Uncle Jim, a co-op shop manager in Bourne, managed to find a temporary job for me working with an auctioneer who was very busy selling off the premises, stock and plant of farmers who had gone bankrupt. I was paid thirty shillings a week and, as I lived with my uncle who would not take any money off me for my board and lodging, I was able to send a little over one pound a week to Lincoln where my mother, again out of work, was living with my younger sister. The sick clerk whom I had temporarily replaced made a miraculous recovery so it was not long before I was again both home in Lincoln, and back in the dole queue, and once more involved with the Labour League of Youth and the WEA. At this time considerable coverage was being given in the national press to the proceedings of the Great Disarmament Conference in Geneva and posters appeared carrying the dove of peace and appealing for the abolition of warfare as a means of settling international disputes. The pacifist within me was sufficiently stirred for me to join the No More War Movement where I met a lot of men much older than myself who had been conscientious objectors in the First World War. They had endured severe hardships for their beliefs, and many had no index fingers on their right hand, having voluntarily cut off the trigger finger so that they could not be called upon to fire a gun. My admiration for these men was unlimited especially for George Deer who was later to become the Member of Parliament for Newark.

Gradually, however, my enthusiasm for the pacifist cause and my admiration for those who played so prominent a part in advocating its ideals began to weaken. Increasingly I became aware that in Italy, Germany and Japan there was emerging more vigorously with each passing day a doctrine of Fascism that would eventually have to be met with force if its triumphant progress was to be arrested. In the face of such an expansionist and vicious ideology, pacifism seemed unable to offer either a viable alternative or a definitive answer. I became ever more convinced that if Fascism was to be contained or better still eradicated, then only a show of armed resolve and a clearly stated preparedness to meet military might with military might could save the world from suffering and languishing under such a despicable and reactionary creed.

My membership of the No More War Movement ended shortly after one of my last meetings with George Deer who had been its mainstay in Lincoln for many years, and who had himself endured terrible privations for his refusal to fight for 'King and Country' against fellow members of the working-class in the First World War. That meeting, which took place

just as I was about to set off with the north-east contingent on the Hunger March to London in early 1934, left me sadly disillusioned with the man whom I had so very much admired. As I and a few others from Lincoln prepared to join the column of marching men George stepped over to us, but far from offering the expected words of encouragement he was disparaging of our intentions. 'What good are you going to do by marching to London?' he asked. 'You're just going with a collecting-box, bumming your way to London. What effect do you think you're going to have even if you do eventually get there? People are laughing at you.' Although I was shocked and hurt by George's words, with hindsight, I can now appreciate his feelings. He had enjoyed a long career as a trade union official and had been a devoted supporter of the Labour Party for all his adult life and it was thus not too surprising that he was opposed to those who joined a march organized by the National Unemployed Workers' Movement, an organization which had many disagreements with both the Trades Union Congress and the Labour Party. At the time, however, George's words cut deep, and although we were to talk together on future occasions I could never recapture my former regard for him, and our subsequent conversations developed rapidly into heated arguments. It seemed as I moved increasingly towards the left of the political spectrum George was setting sail toward the right, and the gulf between us widened with every change in the nation's domestic and international political life.

My circle of friends was more and more drawn from among those who were in some way active in political organizations, and continuing unemployment throughout 1933 drew that circle ever more tightly together as politics became an integral part of my daily existence. Compared with the political battle all else appeared humdrum and mundane. Yet it was 1934 which really converted me into a radical, for one of the great marches of the unemployed organized by the National Unemployed Workers Movement took place, with a contingent of marchers passing through Lincoln.

There can be no question but that the NUWM was by far the most important organization of the unemployed during the years of economic stagnation, but it is often forgotten that it had been founded in 1921 as a militant organization to campaign on behalf of the unemployed. Talk of the hunger marches of the 1930s today inevitably calls forth recollections of the Jarrow Hunger March, or Jarrow Crusade of 1936, organized by the MP for Jarrow, Ellen Wilkinson, and the Mayor and Council. It is often overlooked that the Jarrow march was but one of many marches, and was unique in that it was the only march in the 1930s not organized by the

NUWM. From its origin the NUWM had strong links with the Communist Party of Great Britain. Walter Hannington was the NUWM's most important leader and spokesman and, as he had been a founder member of the CPGB, it was inevitable that the two organizations should share a common orientation. From the outset the NUWM revealed its radical nature by vigorously campaigning for concessions to be made on relief scales, by being active in support of strikes and by lending support to picket lines and in trying to dissuade the unemployed from acting as blackleg labour.

I first became aware of the NUWM through reading its fortnightly paper, *Out of Work*, and was immediately impressed by its radical campaigning zeal. It seemed to me that the NUWM was the only organization which had any real interest in improving the lot of the unemployed, and had staged a national hunger march, the first of its kind, as early as 1922 with contingents of unemployed workers marching on London from the depressed areas. This highly visible means of protest was to be repeated time and again by the NUWM as the employment situation worsened in the late 1920s and into the 1930s. My imagination was captured and retained in 1932, when the NUWM called the 'Great National Hunger March against the Means Test' with eighteen contingents from all parts of England, Scotland and Wales, setting off to London where they were to meet on 27th October, hold meetings, present a petition of a million signatures against the means test and demand the restoration of the ten per cent cut in unemployment benefit introduced by the National Government. The outbreaks of violence which occurred once the marchers had reached London and the universal condemnation which the march provoked in Parliament, especially that from the Home Secretary, Sir John Gilmour, and in the national press, convinced me still more that the NUWM was indeed the only organization with a real interest in helping the unemployed and stood virtually alone in the battle to improve the position of the working class.

When, in 1934, the NUWM announced that it was to stage another hunger march with contingents representing all of the depressed areas timed to converge simultaneously upon London, and when it became known that the Tyneside contingent was to pass through Lincoln, my enthusiasm for the NUWM cause reached new heights, for my experience of unemployment had left me bitter and ready to seek some form of revenge against a government, which treated the unemployed with such obvious and callous disdain. In Lincoln preparations were made to receive the marchers. The Trade Council equipped, as best as it

could, some derelict school buildings to provide over-night accommodation, and collections were taken to provide food and a few small luxuries
like tobacco and clean socks. Also a list was circulated calling for
volunteers to join the march at Lincoln. I was one of the initiators of this
list. My mother's reaction when I told her that I was going to march to
London was one of incredulity, but my obvious resolve convinced her that
I was not treating the matter lightly and would be with the march when it
set off on its next stage to the south. When the marchers reached Lincoln
they held a meeting and a number of them addressed the crowd which had
gathered to greet them. Some of the marchers had given speeches all the
way from Tyneside and what speakers they were! Constant practice had
given them a full command of impromptu speech-making before strange
audiences in different market squares. They thought nothing of delivering terrific, rousing speeches off the cuff and after listening to them
nothing would have made me change my mind to walk to London in their
company. So the next morning when the march set off I, and perhaps six
others from Lincoln, fell into step.

The Tyneside contingent was under the leadership of a Communist
councillor, Bobbie Elliott. Office-holding, and the power by which it is
accompanied, is frequently said to make people less radical and more
conservative and uncaring for the plight of others. In Bobbie Elliott's case
such a charge was fatuous. Never for a moment did Bobbie lose touch
with those whose ideals he shared. He worked many minor miracles on
that march to London, ensuring that men who were far from being in peak
physical condition after months of unemployment and a poor diet, kept on
walking through the winter weather. I was to meet Bobbie again in Spain
where he served with the Republican forces as a political commissar, a job
for which his past experience as a doughty political fighter and an
organizer of radical forms of political protest equipped him admirably.

Bobbie's immediate subordinate on the march was Wilf Jobling. Wilf
was an extremely attractive personality. He was athletically built, with a
powerful voice, which was ideal for addressing open-air meetings, and a
wonderfully persuasive magnetism. Tirelessly Wilf would walk up and
down the length of the marching column of shabbily dressed and weary
men, urging them on with words of encouragement and offering advice on
how to treat tired and blistered feet. Like Bobbie, Wilf was to fight in
Spain against the Nationalists and it was a great loss to the cause of
working-class radicalism in Britain that both of them were killed in 1937
within a few months of each other: Wilf at Jarama in February, Bobbie at
Brunete in July.

The marchers had a seemingly endless repertoire of songs which they sang to bolster flagging spirits and exhausted bodies. Many were translations of Red Army and Soviet revolutionary ballads and it was on the march that I learnt the stirring words of 'The Internationale'. We marched in the middle of an English winter in shoes ill-equipped to take the daily pounding meted out to them by the metalled road surfaces. Our clothes already bore the signs of age, for months and in many cases years of unemployment were not conducive to sartorial elegance. If we were scruffy we were also less than fragrant, for regular drenching in winter showers of rain, sleet and snow and inadequate washing facilities meant that hot soapy water was a rare luxury. Offsetting the hardships of the daily march and the discomfort of the winter weather was the warmth of the reception at each night's resting place. Sleeping accommodation was invariably the wooden floor of a church hall or some other building which had been pressed into temporary service, but the feeling of comradeship, sympathy and understanding emanating from our hosts made the rigours of the daily march, the unyielding hardness of a wooden bed, and the coarseness of a single blanket seem a small price to pay for membership in such a marvellous band of men. What men they were! Even well-fed and well-trained troops accustomed to lengthy marches would have grumbled bitterly at marching day after day in winter, but not these men. With no training and only the clothes in which they stood and having enjoyed little good food they never voiced a word of complaint. Each morning they shook the aches and stiffness from their joints and fell cheerfully into line. On the march they sang and swapped stories, told jokes, discussed politics both domestic and international, encouraged each other to keep on walking, and especially they tried to raise the spirits of those upon whom the daily rigours were taking their toll. But never a word of complaint or self-pity passed their lips. Some, for whom the march proved more than their physique could withstand, had to be sent home by train and Bobbie Elliott and Wilf Jobling saw that this was done. No recrimination was voiced, never were those who had to leave the march made to feel that they had failed or that they had let others down.

As the column approached London it was probably not more than two hundred strong and it excited more curiosity than interest as it threaded its way through the prosperous suburbs but, as it crossed the working-class districts on its way to the centre, people came out of their houses and thronged the pavements shouting encouragement. Many Londoners actually joined the column and at a meeting in Hyde Park on the following day tens of thousands were present to listen to the speeches. I was too

tired to think of pushing and shoving my way to the front of such a vast gathering to hear the speeches and chose instead to stretch out on the grass some distance away and catch up on some long-overdue sleep!

In all I spent the best part of a week in London and although some previous NUWM marches to the capital had produced isolated, violent clashes with the police I can recall only one occasion on which things got a little out of hand and the mood of the marchers became, uncharacteristically, ugly. It had been arranged in advance that those of us who had come south with the column would spend a day at the House of Commons lobbying our respective members of parliament and seeking to draw their attention, yet again, to the hardships and misery which unemployment caused not only to the unemployed themselves but also to their families, indeed, to entire communities and regions. For some reason that was never entirely clear fighting broke out between ourselves and the police. A baton charge by the police, we called them 'Trenchard's Cossacks' after their chief, resulted in several marchers receiving cuts and bruises and others being arrested for causing a disturbance. Considering the numbers involved and the strength of feeling, the fighting was insignificant, although it undoubtedly added to the 'bad press' which NUWM marches inevitably attracted, and gave further support to the establishment's perception of the marchers as idle, left-wing hooligans bent on fomenting trouble. Nothing, of course, could have been further from the truth. True the marchers were idle, but not from choice. True they were predominantly left-wing but given their circumstances this was not really too surprising.

Despite my mother's hopes, she failed to divert me from my political activities by moving the family to Bulwell. If anything she achieved the exact opposite of what she had intended. All that I saw in Bulwell raised my political temperature to near boiling-point. It was a village dependent on its coal-mine and it was a derelict place of derelict men. There were dozens and dozens of men standing around, grey and poverty-stricken. The old pit militants had not worked since 1926 and had endured eight years of continuous unemployment. The village had many old stone cottages that were on the verge of collapse and the entire community and its inhabitants bore the stamp of suffering and neglect. It was a dreadful place. Poverty was more visible in Bulwell than ever it had been in Lincoln. No middle-class person would ever have chosen to live there amid such physical squalor and human misery. In the circumstances it was not surprising that I lost no time in joining the local branch of the NUWM and, as I moved rapidly further to the left of the political

continuum, I was shortly seeking membership of the Communist Party. Extreme poverty required an extreme solution, and hence organizations considered by many to be extremist in nature flourished amid the human and material dereliction which characterized Bulwell.

Although by the middle of 1934 many commentators thought the worst of the recession was over, such pronouncements made no appreciable difference to Bulwell and its inhabitants and, encouraged by my mother's constant appeals to make something of myself and my life by leaving my political activities and finding work, I decided to join the Army which seemed to offer the only source of income which was open to me. As a volunteer in the Royal Army Service Corps I was sent to Aldershot, like generations of volunteers before me, to undergo basic training. However, my army career was to be brief, for despite the fact that I acquired one useful skill, how to care for, aim and shoot a rifle, I failed, of all things, the clerical examination! With so many seeking to avoid unemployment by joining the armed forces, this failure led to my being discharged. What little I did experience of army life proved enjoyable, in particular, the comradeship of my fellow volunteers. That I spent a part of each evening by the barrack-room stove reading the *Daily Worker* and trying to explain what I thought was the political significance of the Asturian Uprising in Spain met with a good deal of leg-pulling and ribald humour. To some extent I suppose I went near to earning the title of 'barrack-room crank', but all of the comments amounted to nothing more than well-intentioned and light-hearted criticism, and neither my fellow volunteers nor my superior officers seemed in the least troubled by my left-wing political views and affiliations. My sojourn in His Majesty's Armed Forces having been prematurely terminated, I returned to Bulwell with some feeling of sadness for I was sure that I could have taken to army life.

By the end of 1934 Fascism, which had until then been largely restricted to the Continent and Japan, made its ugly encroachment ever more strongly into Britain. Nottingham did not escape its clutches, and when a branch of the British Union of Fascists was established in the city, I became involved in attempts to disrupt its programme. I sustained what could be called my first wound in my fight against Fascism on the occasion of a visit by Oswald Mosley to the Victoria Baths. The Communist Party's tactics at Fascist public meetings were basically simple: get as many members as possible into the meeting and then, once it was in progress, cause such disruption that the meeting could no longer continue or the disturbance would have to be quelled by Fascist stewards. Mosley's meeting at the Victoria Baths followed that pattern. Along with several

other comrades I managed to gain admittance, while, outside, a large, hostile crowd assembled, hurling abuse at those entering the Baths and shouting slogans. Mosley was a provocative and rousing speaker and the impact of his personality and words was heightened by the way in which the meeting was orchestrated. As Mosley walked along a corridor through the applauding audience to a platform which had been erected at the far end of the Baths, the lights were dimmed. The platform from which he spoke was devoid of furniture: Mosley stood against a black backdrop illuminated by a solitary spotlight. It was the same technique devised by Goebels for Hitler at Nuremberg, except that a shortage of funds meant that Mosley's meetings were but a poor reflection of the real thing.

After we had begun to shout him down, fighting broke out all over the Baths. While I was trading punches with a member of the audience, a steward attacked me from behind with a folding chair. Fortunately for me its seat was the first part to come into contact with my head, and as it was made of relatively flimsy cane, my head proved to be more than a match for it. Unfortunately, its sturdier wooden frame descended next, only to come into direct conflict with the bridge of my nose: a part of my anatomy which failed miserably to offer anything other than token resistance before blood spread across my face and poured on to my opponents' black shirts. Hospital treatment for my injury took a while to obtain, as on leaving the Baths with further encouragement from the stewards, I had to pass through the police cordon holding back the hostile crowd outside. Next I had to find a passage through the crowd itself which proved far from easy for many assumed that I was a Fascist! So it was a few hours later that I received medical attention at a nearby hospital; this involved removing the bone from my nose, and to this day my nose has assumed a more expansive shape than ever it possessed before Mosley's visit to the Victoria Baths.

Whether or not the police checked with the local hospitals for the names and addresses of those receiving treatment after Mosley's meeting I do not know, but from then on I was a marked man in the eyes of the constabulary whenever a Fascist meeting took place. To cite but one instance of this: when a little-known Fascist speaker called William Joyce came to address a meeting of the BUF at a school in West Bridgford, I was refused admittance by the police. Thus I was deprived of my only opportunity to listen in person to the voice of a man whose words I was to hear over the radio on many further occasions when he was broadcasting from Germany in the Second World War. Certainly at the time of his visit to West Bridgford I am sure that neither I nor Lord Haw-Haw could have guessed at his future career or the fate which awaited him at the war's end.

The attempts in which I was involved to disrupt Fascist meetings had little effect upon the fortunes of the Fascist cause in Britain. Communist Party members and others of a left-wing political persuasion undoubtedly succeeded in cutting short many of the Fascists' public gatherings, but our activities were more of nuisance-value than of any political significance. Mosley failed because he never managed to capture the sort of support that would have given him electoral victory. The right wing of the Tory Party never showed him any respect and the working-class at that time, which I am sure was far more politically aware than ever it is today, discerned his real intentions from the outset. Mosley was obliged to seek support from the young, hooligan element who found the status they so eagerly craved by dressing in para-military uniforms, and an outlet for their aggressive tendencies in fighting anyone who opposed them. I suppose in one respect I was not too dissimilar from a youthful supporter of Mosley in that I was ready for trouble and not at all loath to put my fists into action whenever the occasion arose. To many dispassionate onlookers I must have appeared to be no better or worse that the Fascists whom I looked upon as my class enemies, and whom I was pledged to resist and overthrow, but our campaigning built up a revulsion for Fascism which has lasted to this day.

The BUF was not the only political party active in the Nottingham area at that time. The Communist Party was also very much to the fore in seeking to draw the attention of the British working-class to issues of international and national importance – such as the Japanese invasion of Manchuria, Mussolini's armed aggression in Abyssinia and the plight of the unemployed in Britain. Nor was the BUF the only party to make use of Nottingham's Victoria Baths for public meetings as on several occasions the Communist Party used it as a venue for public rallies addressed by Harry Pollitt. Harry was a marvellous speaker and on his visits to Nottingham we could always count on every available seat being occupied at any meeting at which he spoke. He had an extraordinarily powerful voice and it had to be a very big meeting for Harry to have recourse to a microphone. He was an exceptional leader and if at that time the Communist Party was organizationally weak it was not because of any failure on Harry's part. He worked unceasingly to further the Party's cause and under his guidance it reached the peak of its popularity, though never attaining a position from which to challenge the electoral strength of its established political rivals. I met Harry on a number of occasions when I was fighting with the International Brigade in Spain, when he would come to the British Battalion and talk to us of events back home, and tell

us how the activities of the Spanish Aid Committee were progressing. After one visit to the Battalion, Harry quoted me in a broadcast on Radio Moscow; but I only learnt of this many years later. My final meeting with Harry was at Chatham during the Second World War when he addressed a meeting of Chatham trade unionists and, although I was in naval uniform, I went along to listen to him speak. As he left the meeting he gave me a long hard look, as though my face struck him as being familiar, but I made no attempt to talk to him as I was sure that all such meetings were certain to be watched by the authorities.

On a day-to-day basis, the Communist Party in Nottingham owed an inestimable debt to one of its founders, Ernest Kant, who had made the city his home. Ernest had a record of lifelong service to the working class and had been imprisoned just before the General Strike of 1926 when the Government thought that it was facing a revolutionary situation and panicked a little. I am unsure as to the charge on which Ernest was arrested, but I am certain that one would have been dreamed up to ensure if not to justify his incarceration. Ernest had held a great variety of jobs but what really singled him out was that he had spent a long time working in the Soviet Union where he had met all of the major political figures. He had known Lenin, Trotsky and Stalin personally. He brought an immediacy to our knowledge of all things Soviet which we would otherwise have lacked, since our only regular source of information on the developments in Russia, especially the attempts to industrialize under Stalin's first Five Year Plan, was gleaned from a cheap but cheerful magazine called *Russia Today*, which was produced by the 'Friends of the Soviet Union'. This magazine gave a wonderful account of the social and economic developments taking place in the world's only 'people's state', and without exception we in the CPGB were firmly and resolutely behind everything that the Soviet Union was attempting to achieve. No doubt we were all too naïve and idealistic, for we sought to justify even the worst excesses of Stalin's rule: the purges which began in 1935. Although there was really scant justification that could be offered for such cruelty, no matter what objective was being sought, we tended either to acquiesce too quietly, or contend that it was simply an attempt by the establishment press to discredit the Soviet Union.

Even though the political, economic and social climates in the early and mid–1930s were conducive to left-wing radicalism, the Communist Party never succeeded in gaining any significant measure of support from the British working class. Whether this was because of the innate conservatism of the working man, the stranglehold which the pro-establishment

press managed so ably to maintain on all political issues, or because of the Party's strong association with Moscow, I do not know, but the cumulative effect of all these factors obviously worked to the detriment of the Party, so that, for instance, the Nottingham Branch never had a membership in excess of one hundred, even at the time when the depression was at its most severe. Invariably on the agenda for our regular branch meetings were the tactics to be pursued by the NUWM, and by individual trade union local branches in which party members were active; assessments of the international situation which we viewed with ever-growing pessimism after Hitler's installation in Germany, as Mussolini was allowed a free hand in Abyssinia, and as the British Government seemed to sit idly on the side lines and offer no resistance to the aggressive march of Fascism. I thought at that time, and still do think, that of all the British political parties only the Communist Party really understood the international political scene in the 1930s and had any idea of the sort of future which Europe and the world had before them.

It was around the time of the 1935 election that I met Willie Gallacher. He had come to Nottingham to address a public meeting and, having nowhere to stay, spent the night at my home. This caused some anxiety in the family for never before had such a well-known figure crossed our doorstep. My mother was especially alarmed at being called upon to act as hostess to such a national figure, and went to great lengths to see that he could want for nothing, and that he would be made as comfortable as possible. Willie quickly put her mind at rest on his arrival. A short man, a good deal older than me, and with a heavy Scottish accent, he quickly charmed my mother with his polite and gentle manner, despite the fact that politically they were poles apart. There was a dynamism about Willie which is hard to describe but which anyone who had met him would recognize. Perhaps the word 'charismatic', although much overused these days, is the one which affords the most apt description of him. Yet personality alone would not have gained him a seat at Westminster as a Communist, not even in the 1930s, and not even for a mining constituency. To win the votes of the miners, as he did, he would have had to have shown that he was not only worthy of their trust, for to vote for him they would have had to turn their backs on the Labour Party, but also that he truly had their interests at heart. Willie was an altogether remarkable man and I shall never forget the evening we spent together and the clear and concise way in which he portrayed the issues facing the working class and the country as we sat by the fire after supper. There was no hint of condescension or paternalism: he talked but he also listened, he criticized but he never disparaged.

Although committed to left-wing politics which inevitably took the form of public meetings, I never acquired the skills of an orator, but another level of political agitation resulted in my appearance at the local magistrates court. It was my regular practice to go out on to the streets armed with a large chunk of white chalk (the type used in the colliery to mark the coal trucks). With it I would write on the roads such messages as 'Mass Unemployed Demonstration – Leave Bulwell Market 2 p.m. Today', while someone would stand on the pavement to warn me of oncoming vehicles. Although I did little to improve the appearance of the streets I was not doing anything illegal. I deliberately did not write on walls as I was sure that this could have been considered as damage to property, but roads seemed to me a different proposition. However, the Chief Constable of Nottingham in the 1930s had no greater liking for the unemployed of those days than his present-day counterparts appear to have, and determined to put an end to slogan-writing on the streets of his city. One morning as I was busily chalking away I noticed that I was being watched by a police sergeant and a young constable. This had happened before, and we had become sufficiently accustomed to each other's presence that we would now nod to each other although we had not progressed to speaking. This time however, instead of passing by, they followed me as I continued my chalking on different streets. Eventually, the constable parted from his sergeant and joined me.

'Your name please,' he said.

'What's this about?' I answered. 'You know me well enough.'

'Oh,' he said. 'I'll just have your name.'

I gave him my name, he departed, and I carried on chalking. A few days later I received a summons. Chalking on the road was not, as such, illegal, but I was summonsed under a hundred-year-old law which concerned advertising on street corners! Now chalking on street corners was a waste of my time and effort: the constant traffic was too dangerous and also quickly wore away my literary efforts before they could receive the attention I felt they warranted. I always aimed for a straight stretch of road with a nice level surface.

My subsequent court appearance was a disaster! I felt intimidated by the Chairman of the Bench, Alderman John Farr, leader of the Conservative Party in Nottingham and leader of the Conservative Group on the City Council: a political opponent who I felt would show me little understanding and no consideration. Much to my consternation I found myself exhibiting a degree of humility and acquiescence which I did not feel, but which I seemed powerless to shake off. Inevitably, I was found

guilty and fined ten shillings. Fortunately, the fine was paid on my behalf by the NUWM, for I have no idea how I could have raised the money myself.

Within a short time of my court appearance I found a clerical post at the most acceptable wage of two pounds ten shillings per week. This meant that I had to leave the NUWM, which I did with regret, but I joined the Bulwell branch of the National Union of Municipal and General Workers. Nevertheless, paid employment did mean that I had to curtail some of my political activities.

From being a seven-day-a-week political radical I now became a weekend radical. Most of my free time on Saturday afternoons and Sundays was spent canvassing for subscriptions to the *Daily Worker*. The Party badly needed to build up the circulation of its mouthpiece as a means of securing support for its campaigns, but it was severely handicapped in doing so by the refusal of the big newsagents to handle the paper. Bundles of the *Daily Worker* would be put on the train in London as ordinary passenger freight and would be collected from the Midland Station in Nottingham and delivered privately by party members.

As 1935 changed into 1936 I was twenty-three years old and considered myself to be an experienced political campaigner, a radical man of the world. Just how much more experience I was to gain I had no idea, but within a little over twelve months I was to be surprised at the youthful naïveté of that self-portrait: I had a great deal to learn both about life in general and about myself in particular.

Despite talk of nobility and valour, in reality the battlefield is a place where survival is the paramount objective. To survive it is necessary to kill; but often to kill effectively it is necessary to numb the senses and see the enemy as simply a figure that must be eliminated rather than as a fellow member of the human race. In such circumstances even fear can be temporarily suspended for while the tension that precedes a battle can never be overcome, the heat of action and the rapidity of events paralyses the emotions and suspends rationality. Thoughts of pain and death, of the ludicrous risks that are being taken, of the insanity of pitting flesh against metal are thrust from the mind. It is only in those quiet moments that inexplicably arise even in the midst of modern warfare that there is time to assess the enormity of what is happening, recognize the misery and pain that is part and parcel of the business of war and express anger and bitterness at the loss of a close comrade. On such occasions it is possible to appreciate the similar suffering of the enemy and to realize that war as a

means of settling disputes between supposedly civilized people is a most uncivilized undertaking.

Yet I have never regretted my decision to go and fight with the International Brigade in Spain, for there are occasions when principles cannot be pushed aside and sacrifices have to be made. For me the Spanish Civil War was a case in point. Although the war was fought exclusively on Spanish soil, I never saw it as a domestic conflict. To this day I cannot view it except as a part of the struggle between the forces of Fascism and democracy that was being fought throughout Europe. When I served in the British Navy from 1941 onwards and saw service on the North Russian convoys, at the Dieppe raid and during the 'race up the Channel' of the German capital ships (*Prinz Eugen, Scharnhorst* and *Gneisenau*), I always considered that I was simply engaged in a further round of the fight against Fascism which I had entered in 1936.

But the character of the warfare I experienced in Spain was different from what I later endured in the navy. In Spain I was in a foreign land, cut off from home by the vagaries of a chaotic postal service with news reaching me largely through the unceasing efforts of the Battalion's political commissars. In the navy, both on destroyers and in submarines, I never felt so divorced from my family, but nor did I feel so close to my comrades. The British Navy was a microcosm of British society with all of its petty class and status distinctions maintained to the full, especially when it came to relations between officers and other ranks. I often felt that many were in the forces simply because they had no other option and that they understood little of the full implications that failure to secure victory would entail.

In Spain, we were all there not from compulsion but from choice. Our intimacy was genuine, not contrived, and our commitment to the defeat of Fascism was total. We appreciated that it was not an isolated confrontation but part of a wider struggle and indeed Germany and Italy confirmed our suspicion that Franco was being used as an agent of international Fascism by pouring in men and materials to aid the Nationalists. The governments of the western democracies, however, remained wedded to the doctrine of appeasement. Through their naïve trust in the machinations of the Non-Intervention Committee they deluded themselves as to the true nature of the Spanish holocaust until the very end. Only later, almost too late, did they recognize the real character of their opponent, but by then the Spanish Republic was dead. Why were they so blind?

Index

THE SHALLOW GRAVE